# ASSERTION TRAINING

Assertion techniques are not merely concerned with go-getting lifestyles, or with making a spirited defence against sexist or racist behaviour. They are a tool for everyday life, enabling you to enhance your life and to be more effective both personally and professionally.

*Assertion Training* shows how this can be achieved. Being assertive is about being who you really are – and it is also about recognizing and respecting other points of view, not just going for what *you* want at all costs. Using a wealth of illustrative examples and exercises, the authors show how to get in touch with what you want; how to change your negative thought patterns; how to value your own opinions; how to deal with rejection and criticism; and how to build self-esteem and confidence.

Written in an appealing and direct style, *Assertion Training* is intended above all as a practical, self-help guide. It will also be useful to people running their own programmes and will be essential reading for those about to set up their own assertion training groups.

**Shân Rees** is an experienced trainer in personal and professional development and has extensive experience in running Assertion Training courses.

**Roderick Graham** works as a psychologist, teacher and psychotherapist.

# STRATEGIES FOR MENTAL HEALTH

Series editor

**Reinhard Kowalski**
*Principal Clinical Psychologist and Psychotherapist,*
*East Berkshire Health Authority*
*and*
*The Cardinal Clinic, Windsor, Berkshire*

STRATEGIES FOR MENTAL HEALTH is a series of guide books for the mental health practitioner. It will introduce practitioners to relevant therapeutic approaches in a practical 'hands on' way. Over recent years numerous psychological therapy approaches to mental health have been developed and many of them have become well-established methods in the field. The dilemma that practitioners and students face is how to obtain an up-to-date practice-orientated introduction to a particular method without having to work their way through a mass of research literature.

The books in this series are written by experienced practitioners and trainers. Style and content are practice-orientated, giving readers the knowledge, skills, and materials needed to plan, set up, and run projects in their particular area of mental health work. Those who want to acquire a deeper knowledge of the theoretical foundations will find up-to-date references with each of the titles.

*Already published*

*ANXIETY AND STRESS MANAGEMENT*
Trevor J. Powell and Simon J. Enright

*REHABILITATION AND COMMUNITY CARE*
Stephen Pilling

*Forthcoming title*

*BEREAVEMENT AND LOSS*
David Jeffrey

# ASSERTION TRAINING

*How to be who you really are*

SHÂN REES

and

RODERICK S. GRAHAM

TAVISTOCK/ROUTLEDGE
London and New York

First published in 1991
by Routledge
11 New Fetter Lane, London EC4P 4EE

Simultaneously published in the USA and Canada
by Routledge
a division of Routledge, Chapman and Hall Inc.
29 West 35th Street, New York, NY 10001

Reprinted in 1991

Typeset by NWL Editorial Services, Langport, Somerset TA10 9DG

Printed in Great Britain by Mackays of Chatham PLC,
Chatham, Kent

*British Library Cataloguing in Publication Data*
Rees, Shân 1948–
Assertion training: how to be who you really are. –
(Strategies for mental health).
1. Interpersonal relationships. Communication. Assertive behaviour
I. Title. II. Graham, Roderick S. *1944* – III. Series
302.2

*Library of Congress Cataloging in Publication Data*
Rees, Shân 1948–
Assertion training: how to be who you really are/
Shân Rees and Roderick S. Graham.
p.  cm. – (Strategies for mental health)
Includes bibliographical references and index.
1. Assertiveness training. I. Graham, Roderick S., 1944–
II. Title.  III. Series.
RC489.A77G73  1991                                     90–36950
158'.2 – dc20                                          CIP
ISBN 0–415–05816–3
0–415–01073–X (pbk)

With sincere thanks to our clients and students who have shown much courage and wisdom in taking steps towards being who they really are

# CONTENTS

# EDITOR'S INTRODUCTION

The subtitle of this book says it all: 'How to be who you really are'. Shân Rees and Roderick Graham look at assertion and assertiveness training from just that angle: 'How being assertive can help you to become who you really are', rather than 'Use assertiveness skills to become a different, perhaps even better, person'. The subtle difference between the two approaches is not so subtle if we consider the present creative tension that exists between the well-developed cognitive/behavioural approaches and the growing field of humanistic, transpersonal and integrative psychotherapy (see Chapter 2 for a discussion).

Assertion training, like social skills training, has its roots in behaviour therapy with its basic premise that inappropriate behaviour can be unlearned while more appropriate behaviour can be learned. 'Change and growth are possible' is the 'hope message' of the behaviour therapy of the 1970s and 1980s. Things have moved on. We have become used to large-scale changes everywhere, at political, technological, social, interpersonal, and intrapersonal levels. Hence the movement is towards what is most needed to experience and manage all those rapid changes – our values. In the behaviour therapy world the values were only implicit and often muddled. In the humanistic and transpersonal world experience and words are being put to those values.

Shân's and Roderick's book bridges those two worlds: traditional assertion techniques are presented within a growth- and value-orientated context. And the most important message is: deep down you've got it all; assertion techniques can help you to get it out and express who you really are.

This volume is an extremely comprehensive source-book for all those who want to use assertion techniques individually or in groups. All the traditional areas of assertion training are there, from 'saying no' to 'expressing anger'. But throughout the emphasis is on choices, questioning your attitudes, and on expressing yourself as fully as possible. The focus is on finding out what we want to create and how we can go assertively about doing it. Exercises throughout the book help with the different stages: assessing your needs and wants – questioning and reflecting on where they came from and why – making realistic action plans for pursuing what we want – how to go about implementing the plans and how to deal with interferences.

The book is highly relevant clinically, full of examples and case histories (which can be amended and used in teaching and training), and full of experiential exercises. I should like to recommend it to both traditional and alternative counsellors and psychotherapists as a source-book and to others as a structured self-help manual.

Reinhard Kowalski

# Chapter One

# WHAT IS ASSERTION?

'Change occurs when you become who you are, not when you try to become who you are not.'

Being assertive is essentially about respecting yourself and others. It is about having a basic belief that your opinions, beliefs, thoughts and feelings are as important as anybody else's – and that this goes for other people too. It is about being in touch with your own needs and wants, but contrary to some misconceptions about assertive behaviour, it is not about going for what you want at any cost.

To be assertive is to be able to express yourself clearly, directly and appropriately, to value what you think and feel, to have esteem and respect for yourself; to recognize your own strengths and limitations. In other words, to appreciate yourself for who you are. With this as a basis, it is then possible to learn specific techniques which will enable you to change your behaviour in the areas which you choose.

A key word is honesty. It is difficult to be assertive unless you are, first of all, honest with yourself about what you are thinking and feeling. Often when we are speaking to other people, we edit what we want to say, perhaps in order to convey a certain impression, perhaps so that they will not get hurt, perhaps to manipulate them in some way into doing what we want. So the communication is not 'straight'. We shall give lots of examples of these behaviours in the following chapters; take a look at what can happen as a result; and also explore alternative ways of behaving. Basically communicating assertively means telling the truth.

Why are we sometimes reluctant even to tell ourselves the truth about what we are thinking or feeling? Largely because we often do not accept our own thoughts and feelings – we judge ourselves and think we should be other than we are. We shall talk, too, about accepting ourselves, and look at why we do not, if we do not.

Being assertive also means taking responsibility for your life and your choices. It means making your own decisions, rather than simply drifting or going along with other people's choices. It means not blaming other people or 'circumstances' for what happens to you. If you take responsibility for your own life, you can change the parts that are not as you want them. If you blame outside circumstances for your life, it means you are helpless to change it. It is both challenging and exciting to know that we are the creators of our lives – by our own thoughts and actions, we are responsible for what happens to us. How we go about taking more responsibility, and the pay-offs we get when we do not, are also discussed in the following chapters.

When you learn about being assertive, you learn more about yourself, you become more self-aware, because you begin to look at your present behaviour and begin to consider ways of changing it where you want to.

Being actively assertive in the world begins with liking yourself, loving yourself. You can love yourself only if you do not judge yourself in a negative way, as a lot of us do. Liking yourself is not particularly encouraged, at any rate in western society; people are often afraid of relating their accomplishments, in case they are accused of being bigheaded. But if we do not love ourselves, how can we love anybody else, and if we do not love ourselves, why should anybody love us? So we must, first of all, look after ourselves. This does not mean ignoring other people and their needs or wants. We have included in this book many exercises and suggestions to help you to make nourishing yourself part of your life. As with many other things, assertion begins 'at home'. Being assertive towards yourself is an essential first step towards being assertive in other areas of your life.

It is also good to feel confident not only about yourself as an individual, but also about your world. In fact, this naturally follows on from feeling good about 'you'. In general, when people think that negative things are going to 'happen' to them, they do. If we expect to be able to create what we want to, we are more likely to be able to. This expectation will come across in the way we speak, our stance, and the words we use; while we are telling ourselves we are not worthwhile, that we do not deserve to have what we want, then we actually block it happening.

Being assertive is, in a sense, not a big deal. It is our natural way of being which we have lost over the years, and which we can again tune into by being aware of and accepting how we are now, and taking steps towards how we want to be and what we want in the future. Let us now look at an example.

## FRED JONES'S APPOINTMENT

Dr Brown works in a group practice. On a wet Thursday in November he got up late and after an argument with his wife arrived at his surgery about ten minutes late. He had been stuck in heavy traffic. His partner, Dr Merry, had just been called out to see Mr Fairbrother. Mr Fairbrother had a suspected heart attack, so Dr Brown had a double load of patients to see and, by now fifteen minutes late, he settled down to see his first patient. It was five past ten when Fred Jones came in. Fred's appointment had been at nine-thirty and Fred looked unhappy.

Fred had plenty of reasons to look unhappy. He lived with his wife and two children in a fairly crumbly council flat which the council did not seem to want to repair and which Fred had not been able to. Fred's father had recently died. His father had been ill and had lived with them for his last two years. Mary, Fred's wife, had nursed him until he had died of cancer six months ago. About a month ago Fred had found a lump in his chest and he felt worried.

Fred was also concerned about his work, which was making glass-fibre castings. The glass-fibre gave him dermatitis on his forearms. He had seen his doctors about this and their advice was simple. 'Change your job. You are allergic to the glass-fibre.' Fred had said that wasn't on as he needed to work and that was the only work going. So Fred had been prescribed cream. He collected it every three months. Last week he had seen Dr Merry intending to ask him about his lump but it seemed to disappear before he went so he had not mentioned it. His wife had sent him back, and so here he was, having taken time off work again, and he was really worried about being late.

Dr Brown looked up from Fred's notes which he had been reading quickly. 'Sit down, Mr Jones,' he said and then mumbled, 'Sorry you had to wait.' Fred did not hear this: he was looking at his watch.

'How can I help you, Mr Jones?' asked Dr Brown, finally putting down his notes and looking at Fred. Fred felt and looked frozen; 'I've been worried, Doctor,' he said. There was a short silence.

'Yes, yes,' said Dr Brown a little impatiently, glancing at Fred's arms which he thought didn't look as bad as last time. 'It's the arms, isn't it? Well, you know what I told you last time. If you keep working with the fibre you are going to keep getting the dermatitis. I can give you some more cream. I'm sorry, that's all I can do for you.'

Fred did not say anything. Dr Brown wrote out a prescription and handed it to Fred saying, 'Well, there you are then. Take care of yourself.'

Fred did not move for a moment. Dr Brown looked at him and said, 'There wasn't anything else, was there?'

'No,' said Fred hesitatingly.

'Well, there you are then. Take care of yourself,' repeated Dr Brown. He hastily scribbled a note on the end of Fred's file and buzzed for the next patient.

Fred felt unhappy. He now had a prescription which he neither wanted nor needed and still had a lump which he felt worried about. When he arrived at work his foreman greeted him with, 'Hey, Fred. You going to the doctor every week then? What's his receptionist like?'

When Fred got home from work Mary asked, 'How did it go then, dear? Nothing to worry about, was it?'

'Um, no, not really. Don't think so,' said Fred. That did not sound quite right to Mary.

'What did Dr Brown say then?' she asked. 'He did say it wasn't anything to worry about?'

'Um, yes it's OK!' said Fred, a little sharply.

Dr Brown had had a busy and an irritating morning. He dealt with his own and Dr Merry's patients. Dr Merry arrived just as he was finishing. 'Old Fairbrother died,' he said. 'Sorry I'm late. Took a while clearing up there, you understand.'

Dr Brown thought that Dr Merry had been longer than necessary, but did not say anything. Dr Merry looked through the notes. 'Hey!' he exclaimed. 'You've given Fred Jones more cream. Must be eating the stuff. I gave him some only last week.'

'Oh, bother it!' thought Dr Brown. 'Oh, is that so?' he asked. 'I wonder what he was after this morning. He certainly wasn't going to tell me.'

### Consideration of Fred Jones's case

Let us look at alternative ways of behaving which would mean that Fred would be more likely to get what he wanted.

Fred might have felt that he had the right to tell his doctor what he was really worried about. He could have established clearly in his mind before the visit what his purpose was in going to see the doctor. He could have felt that he had a responsibility to look after himself (that no one else was going to do that for him). He might then have asked directly for what he wanted, i.e. advice on his lump.

But Fred did not do any of these things. There must have been some pay-off for him in acting the way he did – we do not do anything for nothing. One pay-off, or advantage, for Fred in failing to ask the doctor what he wanted to ask him was that he avoided feeling uncomfortable; he maintained his usual behaviour and did not take responsibility for saying what he wanted to say; he did not take any risks. It is questionable as to what extent these are advantages in the long term.

The advantages of behaving differently – more assertively – might have been that he had more respect for himself, expressed his needs and therefore created the likelihood of having them met; he might have had the satisfaction of following through a plan and obtaining the intended result. We may note that, through failing to be assertive and express his need to Dr Brown, Fred also caused trouble for himself at work and at home, with his wife.

Dr Brown could have acted differently, to more effect. Instead of reacting to having a full surgery and feeling rushed, he could have been more sensitive to Fred, and afterwards he could have tackled Dr Merry on his lateness. Thus he too maintained the status quo by not stepping outside his customary behaviour.

One of the reasons that both Fred and Dr Brown behaved in the way that they did is that they were giving themselves negative messages. They were telling themselves things and acting accordingly. For example Fred was saying things like, 'I'm not important, what I have to say isn't important. The doctor won't have time to listen to me – I'm not worth listening to. I won't be able to say what I want to clearly.' Doctor Brown might have been saying things like, 'They'll get cross if I keep them waiting too long. They won't like me. I'm a bad doctor' and 'I can't question Dr Merry – he's been here longer than I have.'

We are constantly giving ourselves messages, although we may not realize it. And what we tell ourselves influences what actually happens, e.g. if I go into a room full of people I don't know and I tell myself that no one is going to be interested in talking with me, that no one will find me interesting, I will convey this thought through my body language, through my stance, through my whole way of being. This will tend to be a self-fulfilling prophecy.

If I seem defensive, people are less likely to want to talk with me. Whereas if I go into the room with the positive thought, 'I'm an interesting person, so people will be interested in me, I expect to have a good time here', I will be sending out this message both in my body language and tone of voice and will thus be likely to create a positive situation for myself.

Here is an exercise which will help you to identify messages you give yourself.

Exercise 1.1

1. Remember a situation or incident in the past which did not go well for you.
2. Recall what you were telling yourself while this situation was happening. Write it down.
3. Evaluate it. Ask yourself, not whether what you were telling yourself was 'right', but rather was what you were telling yourself helping you in that situation. Was it helping?
   - your feelings
   - your level of stress
   - your self-esteem
   - your behaviour
   - your relationships
4. If it was not helping you, why were you saying it? Find an alternative message which would be helpful (the opposite of what you were saying). So if you were saying 'I'm not going to be able to do this' an alternative message might be 'I

accomplish this task with ease and confidence.'
5. Next time you are in a similar circumstance, say the positive message to yourself.

At first, you may find it difficult to recall what you have been telling yourself. With practice, you will be able to notice what you are telling yourself at the time it is happening.

The reversing of a negative belief is called an affirmation. If we are looking at a situation from only the negative side, saying affirmations enables us to take a more balanced view. When we give ourselves negative messages, we are usually not telling ourselves the truth about what is happening. Making affirmations helps us to tune in to the positive side. Affirmations should be short and simple and should reverse the negative belief behind the first statement. The words need to feel right for you and it is good if it is a little 'over the top', and makes you smile or laugh, thus indicating something has shifted in your consciousness.

Here is another exercise to increase your self-awareness:

Exercise 1.2

Ask yourself:

– What is happening at this moment?
– What is happening in my body?
– What thoughts are going through my head?
– How am I feeling?

Just notice what the answer is to these questions; do not judge, just notice.

A first step in making any changes we want to make in our behaviour is to be aware of how we behave now, and also, very importantly, to accept it – not to judge or condemn. So a vital ingredient of assertive behaviour is having positive thoughts about ourselves, holding ourselves in sufficient esteem so that we believe that what we think, feel or say is important. The more we are able to do this, the more we shall create positive circumstances for ourselves.

# Chapter Two

# THEORETICAL ASPECTS OF ASSERTION TRAINING

Assertive behaviour is behaviour which enables a person to have the best chance of obtaining their desired results while retaining self-respect and respecting others. 'Assertion' or 'Assertiveness'? These terms are synonymous and are used interchangeably in this book.

## TRAINING OR THERAPY

Assertion training was originally a technique of behaviour therapy and is still practised as such by some psychologists. Most assertion training nowadays involves the inclusion of techniques from humanistic psychology; the ethical value system is often humanistic. Assertion training then is a training rather than a therapy; in particular it is not an insight psychotherapy. The focus in assertiveness training is on the learning of techniques, not on explanations as to how, or why, a person's behaviour is the way it is.

## HISTORY AND DEVELOPMENT

The historical origin of assertiveness training is in behavioural psychology: the work of Pavlov, Salter and Wolpe. It has been further developed by Alberti, Emmonds, Lazarus and Fensterheim. This development has consisted of the observation, isolation, analysis and classification of those behaviours which are assertive. This work has been followed by the evolution of effective techniques for teaching these behaviours. Clearly, assertive behaviour has not been invented; it was part of human behaviour long before the term 'assertive' was applied to it.

In order to understand the history and development of assertion training, we need first to consider the work of the Russian physiologist, Ivan Pavlov (1849–1939). Pavlov was responsible for extensive research into the nature and workings of the nervous system. As a biologist he was interested in the ways in which a living organism adapted to its environment. In higher organisms, including humans, one of the important ways of doing this is through the agency of the nervous system. As a person's environment changes, they too may need to change; otherwise they may experience difficulties.

Pavlov (1927) discovered and described two elements in nervous activity – excitation and inhibition. Excitation involves heightened activity, including the ability to learn new responses. Inhibition is a process decreasing both activity and the ability to learn new responses.

Andrew Salter wrote a classic work on behaviour therapy, *Conditioned Reflex Therapy* (1949). Salter uses Pavlovian concepts of excitation and inhibition, together with other aspects of learning theory, to describe effective behavoural treatments for a variety of disorders. Salter's aim was to increase the excitatory behaviour in a person, enabling them to interact more effectively with their world and to learn more effective ways of interaction. Increase in excitatory behaviour leads to increase in excitatory feelings, as the person becomes more assertive. Salter did not, however, use the term 'assertive' in his work.

Joseph Wolpe was the first worker in this field to use the term 'assertive' (Wolpe 1958). Wolpe found that a person could not experience two contradictory emotional states at the same time. Thus someone could not be relaxed and anxious simultaneously. This is named the Reciprocal Inhibition Principle. Wolpe would encourage his client to relax, and advise his client on ways of doing this, in the face of the anxiety-producing stimuli. This was found to be much more effective than simply trying not to be anxious. It is easier to be something, than to try not to be something. This is the behavioural technique of systematic desensitization, which is used with particular effect in the treatment of phobic conditions.

Similarly Wolpe (1958) showed that behaving assertively in situations of anxiety inhibited the anxiety and led to the client finding it easier to behave assertively in these situations. This is a very creative way of behaving. We do not fight the anxiety: we

9

behave assertively and, perhaps to our surprise, the anxiety disappears. Wolpe considered the expression of anger, affection and pleasure as assertive responses.

Alberti and Emmons (1974) were influenced by the humanistic approach of Carl Rogers (1961) as well as the behavioural techniques of Wolpe. They may claim to be the first to present assertion training as a 'behavioural-humanistic concept for helping persons to gain their perfect rights'. They emphasize the importance of developing self-esteem and of including the expression of positive feelings as part of assertion training.

Arnold Lazarus (1971) introduced his 'broad-spectrum behavior therapy' in which he includes humanistic as well as behavioural approaches. He considers assertion merely as standing up for one's rights but accepts expression of affection, pleasure and other positive feelings as part of 'emotional freedom', which he also considers can be taught.

Thus there has not yet been any generally agreed definition as to what constitutes assertive behaviour; research into the effectiveness and theoretical basis of assertion training is therefore difficult. Within training, there are in fact wide differences in procedures used by different trainers.

Apart from these theoretical differences, even if it is agreed which behaviours should be classified as assertive, in a particular situation there may be differences of opinion as to which behaviours satisfy the stated criteria.

From the more practical viewpoint of the assertion trainers themselves these theoretical considerations are of less consequence. Although it might be desirable, it is now not possible to build a fence around the definition of assertion training.

To further complicate matters, assertion training has become both popular and popularized, and sold as the new answer to everything. This marketing operation, with exaggerated claims being made, has led to disappointment when unrealistic expectations have not been fulfilled. It is natural to be enthusiastic about what one is offering but it is unethical to exaggerate the efficacy of any training or treatment, particularly in the psychological fields.

To be assertive may be good for everyone, but some individuals are unable to be taught assertion techniques. Thus certain basic communication skills must be present in clients to enable training to take place, as well as basic levels of self-confidence and lack of anxiety. Also some people may learn assertion techniques successfully and either choose, or find themselves, unable to use these techniques in situations outside the training area. We suggest that these clients have psychological problems rather than simply problems with assertiveness.

Assertiveness training may be and frequently is combined with or followed up by other techniques for personal growth, for example:

1. Body-language awareness leading to work with body-orientated therapies.
2. Role-plays and then work in psychodrama.
3. Awareness of other people's perceptions and so work in sensitivity groups and encounter.
4. Looking at situations in the past where one was, or was not, assertive and hence traditional psychotherapy.

The techniques, which are taught in assertiveness training, include the following areas:

1. Verbal communication.
2. Non-verbal communication.
3. Anxiety reduction and control.
4. Anger reduction and control, and redirection of this energy.
5. Increase in self-esteem.
6. Awareness of self and others in interpersonal situations.
7. Awareness of social and cultural rules of behaviour.

These techniques may be taught by certain professionals, either on an individual basis or (we think more effectively) in small groups.

## ASSERTIVE RIGHTS AND RESPONSIBILITIES

To train or to be trained in assertive behaviour implies that we have the right to practise this behaviour. The claim of this right is a statement we make of our ethical position, our view of freedom and the respect we have for ourselves and others. Assertive rights are basic human rights. Naturally rights also imply responsibilities. We are also aware that our view of these basic human rights must be, in part, a consequence of our culture. We take responsibility for our views which may be described as liberal and humanistic. A useful exercise would be for the reader to make his or her own list, preferably before considering ours. In some American books these are presented as a 'bill' of rights referring by analogy to the Bill of Rights, part of the Constitution of the United States.

### Human assertive rights

1. The right to do anything which does not violate the rights of others.
2. The right to be assertive or non-assertive.
3. The right to make choices.
4. The right to change.
5. The right to control over body, time and possessions.
6. The right to express opinions and beliefs.
7. The right to think well of oneself.
8. The right to make requests.
9. The right to express sexuality.
10. The right to have needs and desires.
11. The right to fantasy.
12. The right to have information.
13. The right to have goods or services which have been paid for.
14. The right to be independent and to be left alone.
15. The right to say no.
16. The right to be treated with respect.

We shall now consider these assertive rights in detail.

1.  The right to do anything which does not violate the rights of others

This is a fundamental right which includes within it several of the rights which follow. It is difficult to believe that we have the right to do as we like and the responsibility to accept the consequences as long as we do not violate the rights of others.

Unfortunately it is not clear what does violate the rights of others. The general views of people within a society change from time to time but a general view does not make a human right.

Smoking was once a generally accepted behaviour in the UK. Now it is a much less tolerated behaviour on the grounds that it violates the rights of others. If it violates the rights of others now, it did then, so what has changed?

## 2. The right to be assertive or non-assertive

Assertion training gives you the opportunity to relate to the world and others in a different way. We think that it is a better way. 'Better' in that you are more likely to create the life you want, attain your goals and enhance your self-respect. We recommend it to you but we do not say that you must be assertive. It is your right to choose to be assertive or non-assertive as you feel appropriate.

## 3. The right to make choices

When we act assertively, we choose what we do. People experience themselves differently – some feel that they are controlled by their environment, history or financial circumstances. All of these are important, but the choice as to how to act remains that of the individual. Assertive people make choices. If you are assertive, you take your circumstances into account, but do not regard circumstances as controlling you. You take responsibility for your life.

## 4. The right to change

People often encourage us to change, pointing out aspects of our behaviour which they do not like and feel that we could improve upon. However when we start to change and grow, by training, taking a new job, deciding to move to a different address or to seek insight through psychotherapy or spiritual practice we may encounter considerable resistance from the very people who encouraged us to change in the first place.

This resistance to our change from others often occurs when people undergo assertion training. Your friends and relations may be critical of the 'new you' which they let you know does not suit them. Fortunately techniques to deal with this kind of negativity are one of the specific matters covered by assertiveness training.

5. The right to control over body, time and possessions

People vary considerably in their physical size and shape as well as in the pigmentation of skin and hair. Some of these are characteristics we are born with, while others reflect our life-styles. We do surely have the right to choose how we alter our body by our life-style, by diet or exercise for example, and this right of control belongs to us, not to others.

Similarly we have the right to choose to spend our time in the way we choose, despite the advice of our friends and relations that we should spend it differently.

Control over possessions seems at first sight to be a readily accepted right in our materialistic society. This illusion soon changes when our friends want to borrow our books, records or car or our relatives object to our giving away our money to charities, money to which they feel they have a moral right.

6. The right to express opinions and beliefs

Were you ever told when you were a child, 'You mustn't say that in front of . . .' or 'You're stupid if you think that!'?

Maybe as children our views were too simple, or perhaps too embarrassingly correct, for our elders. Many of us still carry their negative messages with us into adult life. So we are afraid of expressing our opinions or beliefs, in case we look stupid, or we fear that others will think less of us. Perhaps we may even doubt our right to have opinions and beliefs at all.

But to be human is to have opinions and beliefs. To express these is part of our essential humanity and is, we contend, a basic right of people.

7. The right to think well of oneself

If you do not think well of yourself, why should you expect anyone else to think well of you? Often we tend to depend on other people to give us their approval of our actions or point of view before we approve of ourselves. It is good to learn to have faith in your assessment of yourself. Despite messages we may, perhaps, receive to the contrary in childhood, it is, in fact, your absolute right to think well of yourself.

14

### 8. The right to make requests

'Faint heart never won fair lady.' If we do not ask for what or who we want, then our chances of success are much reduced. It is not fair on others to expect them to read our mind and so perhaps to choose to give us what we want. Likewise we cannot read the minds of others – perhaps they might wish to grant our request. If we are low in self-esteem, and frightened to ask, we ensure our security at the expense of our growth. We do have the right to ask for what we want.

### 9. The right to express sexuality

In our culture people are often brought up to feel anxious about their sexuality and to wonder what is 'right' or 'wrong' in expressing their sexuality. It is sad, but the right to express and enjoy sexuality is one of the most difficult for many people. We take the view that whatever sexual activity consenting adults enjoy in private, on their own or with others, is no business of anybody else.

### 10. The right to have needs and desires

This means no less than that we allow ourselves to want what we want and to accept that we need what we need. For some people used to 'putting others first', recognizing that they themselves have needs and desires, and that these are as important as anybody else's, is an important stage in acquiring personal freedom.

### 11. The right to fantasy

Most of us are able to distinguish quite clearly between fantasy and reality. To live in a world of fantasy is to avoid reality and exchange a real for an unreal world, but to discard fantasy is to deprive ourselves of much creative power and enjoyment. We can choose the right to enjoy our fantasy.

### 12. The right to have information

In order to make meaningful decisions in creating our lives, we need access to information. This may be information about ourselves, such as is contained in medical, social, school or college reports or to employment references. These are essentially the opinions of others with varying degrees of expertise and objectivity. In addition, we need information about health issues, effects and safety of drugs and contraception, similarly for consumer products and foodstuffs.

### 13. The right to have goods or services which have been paid for

This does seem obvious; however, experience of consumers shows that a small number of the providers of goods and services do not really believe that their customers deserve to receive what they have paid for. Many people have assertive difficulties in this area and this is consequently one of the topics which is most popularly covered on assertion training courses.

### 14. The right to be independent and to be left alone

This involves the right to choose to live or work on one's own and to choose to marry or to be involved in a close relationship or not. Importantly it includes the right to maintain one's own individuality in the face of pressure from a group to conform. Also to have privacy in such matters as not answering the front door or the telephone. Finally, to have the right to be able to spend time in solitary walks, prayer or meditation, if that is what one wishes.

### 15. The right to say no

The inability to say no is one of the most frequent problems experienced by non-assertive people. To say no to people when we want to is a very positive and necessary skill. If, for much of our lives, we have said yes when we wanted to say no, we will have undermined ourselves and our self-esteem, perhaps even to the extent that we question whether we have even the right to say no. However, if we do not say no, then we misrepresent ourselves to others; we are in effect dishonest and fail to respect other people or ourselves.

### 16. The right to be treated with respect

To be treated with respect is to be treated as a person, not as a thing. We are all entitled to respect from others, but sometimes we need to remind them of the fact. By and large, people treat us in the way we indicate we expect to be treated. Our right to be respected, as a person, is independent of our race, gender, sexuality, class, religion, profession, wealth or any of the many other ways that human beings have evolved of separating themselves into groups.

16

## ASSERTIVENESS TRAINING AND AMERICAN CULTURE

Assertiveness training is popular in the United States where it was developed. There are cultural differences between the United States and Britain and these need to be considered when American-style 'assertion' is taught in Britain. White middle-class British people have sometimes identified the assertive behaviour of their American counterparts as being aggressive, while Americans have sometimes found it difficult to establish what British people really think or feel. Books written from the point of view of US culture need to be used with care in Britain.

Assertion trainers need to be conversant with, and respectful of, the particular culture within which they are training clients. This said, it may be observed that the norms of the two cultures are presently moving nearer together. Problems occur when people do not know by which cultural rules communications are being made. Is the person operating under British or American cultural and linguistic norms?

## PRESENT POPULARITY OF ASSERTIVENESS TRAINING

Assertiveness training has much increased in popularity over the last decade. Why is this? We suggest the following as some of the reasons:

1. The general questioning of authority and authoritarianism.
2. The rise of the women's movement.
3. Social changes affecting relationships between men and women.
4. The rise of the consumer movement.
5. Relative deprivation as a consequence of economic recession.
6. Mixing of different cultures and the need for adequate communication between them.
7. Interest in the psyche as in the 'Me decade'.
8. The influence of American culture and ideas.

## FUTURE DEVELOPMENTS

Within the strictly scientific field of behavioural psychology, more work needs to be done on defining assertive behaviour, the most effective ways of teaching this behaviour, and the groups who might benefit from this treatment. From the practical point of view of the assertion trainers, various combinations of assertion training will be combined with therapies and educative methods, to give what appears to the trainer the most effective service for the group with which the trainer is working.

We see three areas of development as being of most interest: training to enhance self-esteem, the teaching of how to release the creative potential within clients and the combination of assertion training with counselling and humanistic psychotherapy. These are recurrent themes in this book.

# Chapter Three

# ASSERTION AND
# ALTERNATIVE BEHAVIOURS
## *Managing change*

Is being assertive always the best way of behaving? We think that it usually gives you the best chance of getting where you want to go.

We all display a mixture of behaviours: in some situations we might be passive, in others, aggressive, and in others, assertive. Whatever our behaviour in a particular situation, we are getting something out of behaving in that way: we do not do anything for nothing.

What could be the possible pay-offs of acting other than assertively? First, you may want want to maintain familiar behaviour either because you feel more comfortable with this or because other people do not like you to change, so if you maintain old behaviour, you feel more accepted by them. We want to be accepted. To some extent, we depend on others for our self-esteem.

Second, if you are accustomed to looking after other people and making their needs more important than your own and you begin to get in touch with your own needs, you may feel you are being selfish by contrast with how you usually behave. You might continue to put the other person's needs above your own. As a child, you might have been praised for doing this – particularly if you are female. So you carry on being passive in situations, out of habit, and because you are used to being praised for it.

Third, we may be reluctant to express our opinions, ideas and feelings, if they do not fit in with what is widely regarded as the norm; perhaps you do not like to be thought of as 'different'. In most cultures being different tends to be regarded as negative;

differences are not celebrated. Conforming to the norm tends to be validated, deviating from it frowned upon. So you may feel it saves a lot of hassle if you simply conform. Sometimes it saves trouble in the short term, but it may lead to problems over time.

## DIFFERENT KINDS OF BEHAVIOUR

Let us look more closely at different kinds of behaviour and give some examples.

You have cooked a meal for some friends and have been waiting for them to arrive. You are feeling angry because they are late. They finally arrive, an hour late. Possible responses are:

1. 'Where the hell have you been, the food is ruined!'
2. 'Oh, don't worry, it doesn't matter. Come in, I'll dish up.'
3. 'What happened? Are you all right? I really was getting fed up waiting for you. Let's see if the food is still edible.'

You have promised a friend who has not been well that you will help him with some work in the garden. You have arranged that he will call you when he feels like having a go himself and you will tackle it together. On the day he calls, you are very busy and very tired and do not really have the time. Possible responses are:

1. 'Why didn't you give me more notice?' asked in an irritable tone of voice.
2. 'I'm terribly sorry, I don't think I can today, I'm behind with my work and I've promised to go over to Janet's and I normally call in at my mother's on a Tuesday . . . I'm awfully sorry' and you feel guilty afterwards. Or say 'Oh all right, if you feel like doing it now. . .'
3. 'I'm sorry, I can't manage today – I'll pop in tomorrow and we can arrange a definite time then.'

In the above examples the first responses are aggressive, the second responses passive and the third responses assertive.

In the aggressive responses, there is seemingly no compassion and no acknowledgement of the other people in the situation. The aggressive person has low self-esteem – although this may not be obvious at first sight, this person cannot give much space or concern to other people.

Another form of aggressive behaviour is indirect aggression. Rather than directly blaming the other person, the indirectly aggressive person gives the impression that things are fine, but obviously they are not. In the first example an indirectly aggressive response would be to give response (2) but to make it obvious through body language that you mean something different – that it does matter. Being at the other end of an indirectly aggressive response is usually very uncomfortable: you know that people are angry or that something is going on but they are simply not saying it. If they said what they meant, it would be easier to deal with. This sort of behaviour occurs often because people are over-concerned with self-image – they want to come across as tolerant and 'nice'; of course this backfires, because if you are bottling something up, it comes out anyway, often in the form of resentment.

In the passive responses, you would scarcely be taking yourself into account at all, but making the other person's needs more important than your own. This too would probably end in you feeling resentful later on.

In the assertive reponses, concern has been expressed for the other person or people; you have explained your own position and the consequent action, and made a constructive suggestion for the future.

What are the advantages of this behaviour? What would you gain by behaving assertively? You would be true to yourself, respect yourself and the other person, and acknowledge your feelings. By making a constructive suggestion for the future you would lay the ground for a positive outcome.

Non-assertive behaviour may sometimes serve you in the short term but not in the long term. For example Sue felt she was unassertive with a particular friend with whom she used to go out in the evenings. Her friend always made suggestions as to where they might go. Usually the suggestions were good ones, and Sue was very happy to agree. Occasionally however Sue had a good idea herself, but found herself suppressing it, as she thought her friend would either disagree or have a better idea. (Note: the numbers in parentheses refer to the stages in Exercise 3.1 below.)

Sue asked herself what the pay-offs were for her in acting in this way (2). The answers she came up with were that she did not have to think and could just go along with what happened, and usually ended up enjoying herself reasonably well. The disadvantages (3) were that Sue felt rather undermined and inferior when she went out with this particular friend. What would she gain (4) by being assertive in the situation? More self-esteem, more feeling of strength within herself, more power of choice, even more enjoyment?

Sue decided that the next time she and her friend arranged to go out she would make a conscious effort to come up with an idea herself, and suggest it.

Exercise 3.1 (see Notes, p. 130)

1. Think of a situation in your life where you behave non-assertively.
2. What is/are the pay-off(s) for you in behaving in this way in this situation?
3. What are the disadvantages?
4. Identify what you may gain by being assertive in the situation. Consider the following possibilities:
   - independence
   - self-respect
   - being true to yourself
   - honesty in relationships
   - inner peace
   - clarity.
5. Consciously make a choice whether you want to maintain your old behaviour or whether you want to learn to be assertive in this situation.

Actually making the choice encourages action in the intended direction. Also vague feelings of 'I should do something different' will be minimized. There will no longer be any need for that. You will have thought about it, and made your choice. Remember it is perfectly all right to maintain old behaviours, if that is what you truly want to do. You can choose.

It is necessary to accept how we behave now, at the level of actually acknowledging, telling ourselves the truth about what is happening. We can move forwards only from a point of accepting what our starting-point is. A key to accepting ourselves is to give ourselves positive messages, to appreciate ourselves; the more we appreciate ourselves the less we shall be dependent on others for appreciation, and the more it will feel important to express who we are, rather than who others expect us to be.

Exercise 3.2

1. Write a list of ten things you like about yourself; include abilities, skills, qualities, achievements.
2. Read the list to yourself once a day for a fortnight. Add to it.
3. Each day, notice something positive that you do. It does not have to be a big thing – although it can be. Congratulate yourself.

We are not used to thinking well of ourselves: we need to relearn the habit.

In order to be assertive, we must begin to be in touch with what we really want in life. Often we do not allow ourselves to be in touch with what we want because we are afraid of not getting it.

Exercise 3.3

1. Make a list of things you want. Do not think about or censor what you write. If negative thoughts intrude, e.g. 'I couldn't afford that', or 'That's impossible', just notice them and continue the list.
2. Read through your list and acknowledge what you have written.

This exercise will help you to become clearer about acknowledging what you want, and it is a good idea to repeat it from time to time.

A reason for being reluctant to express ourselves is a feeling of powerlessness which a lot of us feel. This is a big block to expressing who we are. In order to get in touch with a feeling of strength, we must stop blaming others and thus playing the role of victim. We must take responsibility for our lives. If we are blaming other people for what is happening in our life, we cannot change it. If we take responsibility ourselves for what is happening, then we can change it if we want to.

Exercise 3.4 (see Notes, p. 131)

1. Make a list of situations in which you feel powerless or victimized.
2. Focus on one of these situations and see if you can find one step you could take to become more assertive and to take back your power in this situation.

Often we are frightened of change. As we have seen, it is perhaps easier, at any rate in the short term, to stay as we are. The unknown is often thought of as being 'bad'.

Exercise 3.5

1. Recall a time you were about to do something new, which was an unknown quantity – perhaps starting a new course or job, moving to a new town or country.
2. Remember how you felt about it before the event: what kinds of messages were you giving yourself about how it would be – were they negative or positive?
3. What was your actual experience of the event when it happened?
4. Did you allow yourself to be open to how it actually was, or did you continue to focus on your picture of how it would be before the event?
5. To what extent were you actually in the experience, actually a part of it, rather than a fairly objective bystander?

We are often frightened of new situations, new events, new people, because we tell ourselves we are not going to be able to handle it. If we are willing to stretch ourselves, to really expand into who we are, to be ourselves, then we will take risks – leaps or small steps – into the unknown. And we will tell ourselves that we can do it. We will remember our positive experiences from the past, not our negative ones, and we will move beyond what we now think of as our limits. The wonderful thing is that when you move beyond your limits, you expand and you no longer think of them as limits; you can move beyond even further.

This process begins with self-esteem; building yourself up, making a commitment to be positive about yourself and your world, giving up negative thinking to make room for the positive.

## SPECIFIC WAYS OF HANDLING CHANGE

### Experiments

Experiment by taking a small step in a direction which you think may support you. Rather than fantasizing about how something might be, try it out, get some facts. Assess your feelings and thoughts about it. Adjust your behaviour accordingly. If it does not work out, simply do something different. Consider two examples. First, you think you might want to move into the country, but are not sure. As an experiment, you might want to spend a weekend or a few days in the place you have in mind and see what it feels like.

Second, you are thinking of buying a property, but can afford little more than a shoebox on your own. You consider the idea of sharing with someone, but are a little apprehensive about doing so. To take a step in this direction and find out more, you might want to talk to people who have done this, and put an advertisement in the paper. This is an assertive stance: this is taking the matter into your own hands and taking responsibility.

### Attitudes

Do you have a feeling that you 'should' know exactly what action to take in a particular circumstance? Sometimes we tend to think that there is a right and wrong way of doing something, and that, if only we had the key, we could unlock the secret, and know what it is. In most situations, it is our attitude that makes the action 'right' or 'wrong' – i.e. appropriate or inappropriate for us. We tend to look at things in rather conditioned ways. In fact, there are opportunities in whatever action we take – it just seems as if there might be more opportunities in one action than in another. And this again comes back to having self-esteem – if we tell ourselves that we have the resources to cope with whatever comes up, we are more likely to be able to do so than if we give ourselves negative, anxiety-inducing messages.

For example, Joan has a yearning to take some time off to travel. One of the first things that comes into Joan's mind when she contemplates this, feeling that this is maybe not the 'right' action to take, is a concern that when she gets back she will not be able to find a job. But really this is 'jumping the gun'. She will not be the same person when she gets back. She may want different things from a job, and therefore a different job. That is a choice she will make then, not now, ahead of the event. However much she tries to analyse the advantages and disadvantages of taking the actions of going travelling, she will not know what the experience is like until she experiences it. If we want to know how everything is going to be in advance, it means we do not trust ourselves to act responsibly and in a way that is true to ourselves at the time.

The assertive stance is to give making a decision a reasonable amount of consideration, choose which direction to take, commit yourself to focusing on that choice, and proceed along your chosen path without wasting energy on questioning the 'rightness' of your decision. There is a lot of scope in the 'unknown'. While we stop ourselves from venturing outside the known, we do not allow to the surface important parts of ourselves which we do not usually show.

Exercise 3.6

1. Think of a time when you took a risk where you were unsure of the outcome and which turned out well.
2. What did you learn from taking this action which you would not otherwise have known? About yourself, the situation, life in general?

Focus on what you want to achieve, not on the obstacles.

Because we are often afraid of changes, we tend to put a lot of energy into the possible pitfalls, rather than focusing on the end result and assuming there is a possibility of it happening. It is important to accept what is actually happening at the moment, rather than pretending to ourselves that things are worse or better than they are. It is possible to instigate change only from a point of acceptance of where you are now.

Exercise 3.7 (see Notes, p. 131)

1. As an experiment, imagine that everything that happens in your life happens for a reason and that you can learn from everything that occurs to you.
2. How would this affect your attitude towards what you now regard as problems or obstacles? Consider:

    –Your train is crowded and you have to stand. You feel very frustrated and then you start talking to the person next to you and find yourself standing next to a very interesting person. You decide to keep in touch.

    – You are stuck in a traffic jam. This could be viewed as an opportunity to learn to keep calm and manage your own stress.

The main reason for taking this stance would be that it serves you better, that it is more likely to support your goals in life; behaving in this way supports your life goal of being stress-free and relaxed.

We have a choice of whether to view life as a more or less rigid set of rules which we have to struggle to identify and then conform to; or to view it as a playground, a backcloth on which we can carry out our experiments – find out which ways of behaving serve us best.

The former is safe, in a sense, and familiar. But we are less likely to come across new ways of being and doing or find new ideas, if we function in this mode. The latter, while sometimes feeling challenging, allows us more scope for discovering who we really are.

# Chapter Four

# ASSERTION IN THE WORK-PLACE

## THE IMPORTANCE OF WORK

Are you happy in your work? Are you in a job you like? Do you want a better job? Here we present an assertive way of looking at these issues. You can change to the work you want. First let us consider the rewards that people receive from work. These are:

1. Personal identity.
2. Wages or salary.
3. Satisfaction from exercising skills.
4. Satisfaction from helping people.
5. A social environment.

### Personal identity

When we ask someone 'What are you?' they will often answer, 'I'm a nurse' or 'I'm an engineer', or perhaps less assertively, 'I'm only a housewife.' It seems that one of the important ways we have of identifying ourselves is in terms of our occupation.

### Wages or salary

Most of us need to work in order to obtain money to live. The amount we receive is an important factor for many of us in the work we choose to do.

### Satisfaction from exercising skills

A craftsperson who makes or repairs something will have satisfaction and pride in doing so. Thus to make a motor car go, to write a book, to make a dress, to build a house – these are all creative acts.

### Satisfaction from helping people

Here we have jobs like a nurse, social worker, doctor, shop-assistant and receptionist where the main emphasis of the work is to help or serve others in some way.

### A social environment

For many people their work-place is an important place to meet new people, to make friends and acquaintances and to have as a social support as a basis of a social network.

Each job provides a different mix of these work rewards.

*Nurse* a strong sense of personal identity as this occupation is generally recognized and respected, money rewards low, high satisfaction from exercising skills and helping people, and (within a hospital) a social environment.

*Civil Service clerk* sense of identity, money rewards low, satisfaction from exercising skills and helping people (depending on department), social environment variable.

*Motor mechanic* sense of identity, money rewards medium, satisfaction from exercising skills high (depending on specific work), satisfaction from helping people (depending on contact with customers), high in a small garage, low in a large work-place where the mechanic does not meet the customers.

Here is an exercise to focus on your own job. It is not an exercise with 'correct' answers but an opportunity for you to explore your experience.

Exercise 4.1

1. Sit comfortably and relax.
2. Imagine yourself doing your job.
3. What rewards do you get from your work?
4. How important are these rewards to you?
5. Is there anything you would like to be getting from a job which is missing from your present job?
6. Make a list of these things – see the examples above.
7. Consider how you can move from where you are to where you want to be in terms of your work. What assertive skills would you exercise? What might be one small step you could take towards this, for example finding out about vacancies for your ideal job?

Today the demand for work skills is changing with great rapidity in what has been called the post-industrial age. Historically, a son would either learn the same skill as his father, or his father would find him a suitable apprenticeship. He might become, say, a harness-maker or a goldsmith. Women were involved in less skilled work, usually in domestic situations. The demand for skills changed with the increased use of machinery in the Industrial Revolution and now is changing with the increased use of electronics in the computer age. These new electronic methods of working demand new skills as well as rendering old skills obsolete. For example in the newspaper industry, many of the skills of typesetters have now vanished, and their work may be done by electronic typesetting machines which need only a competent typist to operate them. The machines themselves need workers to maintain them, with new skills not previously needed. Similarly in nursing, nurses are acquiring the skills to use complex electronic equipment to monitor patients' progress as well as learning new interpersonal skills in counselling and health education.

Thus nowadays people may need to retrain once or more in their working lives and to pay attention to the development of their career in ways which were unnecessary in previous times. To be aware of, and to plan, one's career is an important assertive skill. This does not apply only to manual skills; some young professionals employed in financial services, who were too busy earning good money, have been taken by surprise to find that the demand for their skills has changed.

There is an assertive orientation towards your working life and career development. This is to regard your career as an ongoing developing process. No longer if you have a degree in, say, chemistry will you simply be a chemist using the same skills to your dying day. When in work it is necessary to appreciate that change is inevitable and it is necessary for you to keep informed of changes in the likely demand for your skill, the way your company is succeeding or otherwise as well as your company's future plans for merger or relocation and your place, if any, in these plans.

Work is task orientated: the primary concern is in defining the tasks to be performed and doing them. This is different from social life where your focus is on enjoyment, self-disclosure, and fulfilling emotional and affiliative needs. At work these needs are secondary to the tasks to be completed.

We all bring our values, needs and prejudices to our work. Problems may arise, however, when people attempt to fulfil inappropriate emotional needs at work, particularly if they are not aware that they are doing so. (Inappropriate in this case means behaving in a way which decreases a person's efficiency as a worker.)

The need to be liked, for example, is an important personal need but in the work-place the need to be respected as a professional is more relevant. If at work your anxiety to be liked leads you to behave less than thoroughly professionally, you are likely not to be respected in terms of your work performance; it is possible that you may be liked but not respected – 'John's a nice chap, but I don't think he can handle anything difficult.' Often if you behave efficiently, assertively and professionally, liking will come as well as respect.

Exercise 4.2

1. Will your place of work be the same in five years' time?
2. Will you still be there, doing the same job?
3. Are you improving your skills and learning new ones?
4. If a chance of promotion came up would you be ready for it?
5. What is the next step in developing your career?

## JOB TITLES AND JOB DESCRIPTIONS

Your job title is simply what your job is called, so if we ask someone, 'What's your job?' and they answer, 'I'm Sister in charge of Ward 10' or 'I'm the electrician' then we have their job title. Job titles may be designed to reflect real or imagined status, so a shop-assistant may become a 'consultant' or a junior clerk a 'trainee manager'.

Job descriptions refer to the nature and extent of duties that your employer may reasonably require you to perform. These have been a cause of conflict in the past with some workers, for example in shipbuilding, where workers insisted on very restrictive job descriptions. Employers in other employment fields, for example in some residential social work, insisted that their employees worked as and when directed. Nowadays most reasonable employers agree with their employees a definite job description before the employee is appointed and negotiate any variations as the need for them arises.

Exercise 4.3

1. Do you have a job description?
2. How far do your actual duties correspond to your job description?
3. Are these responsibilities similar to those of your colleagues on similar grades?

## POWER IN THE WORK-PLACE

Each work-place has a power and hierarchical structure. In order to understand the power relationships at work it is necessary to understand the various types of power which exist.

### Types of power

1. Reward power – the power to give something which another person desires. For example the power of your boss to give you a rise.
2. Coercive power – the power to 'punish'. For example, the power of your boss to deduct money from your pay if you are late.

3. Legitimate power – the power possessed by virtue of a person's position. For example the boss can decide what duties you do.
4. Referent power – the power given us by others because of their emotional response to us of attraction, respect or liking. For example 'I'm sure Nurse George is a good nurse: she's always cheerful and smiling' said by a patient.
5. Expertise power – the power that we have because of our training and competence. For example the power of a plumber to mend a leaking water-pipe, or of a doctor to diagnose an illness.

Exercise 4.4

1. What kinds of power do you exercise at work and outside?
2. What kinds of power do you experience as being exercised over you?
3. What kinds of power would you like to exercise?
4. What kinds of power are you happy to have exercised over you?

*Hierarchies*

The hierarchies, or organizational charts, that exist in every work-place illustrate the responsibilities of workers, for their job performance, one to another. In order to understand how people interact, it is necessary to understand the hierarchies that exist and the position of people within these hierarchies. As well as the formal hierarchies, workers may have additional power depending on such matters as length of service, being the boss's son, being secretary to the boss or being in charge of the switchboard. An understanding of these informal hierarchies is of considerable importance to someone wishing to be successful within an organization.

Assertive skills are needed in dealing with

1. Yourself
2. The manager to whom you report
3. Your colleagues
4. Your subordinates
5. Clients or customers.

Some people have difficulties in dealing assertively with one or more of these groups, while being confident in dealing with members of other groups. This is in part because a person's responsibilities to the members of each of these groups differ.

Exercise 4.5

1. To whom are you responsible for your work?
2. Who is responsible to you?
3. Do you know what your position is in the organization where you work?
4. Do you find it easier to be more assertive towards one or more of the people who belong to the above groups?

We now turn to a consideration of some situations at work which require assertive treatment. They are intended to stimulate thought and discussion and may be used with the preceding exercises as the basis for work with individuals or groups concerned with developing assertion skills in the work-place.

### Jim, the bricklayer

Jim left school at 16 and the one thing he wanted to do was to be a builder. He thought about the various trades he could do and settled on that of a bricklayer. 'Dad,' he said, 'I want to be a bricky. When I see a house built, that's what I see most of, the walls. That's what I want to do.'

So Jim's father had a talk with Mr Minns, the local builder. The outcome of this, over the second round of drinks in the pub one Wednesday evening, was 'Yes, I'm looking for a bricky's mate. I'll take young Jim on and teach him.' The next Monday Jim was working for Mr Minns as a bricky's mate. Jim was very excited. The job he had was to carry the bricks ready for Mr Minns to build and to mix the mortar and have everything to hand and to clear up afterwards. Jim soon got the hang of this and became a quick and efficient worker. He enjoyed his work and all was well for the first six months. By this time Jim was beginning to get a bit impatient because he wanted to build a wall and after all his father had agreed on his behalf that he would be taught to build. One day as Mr Minns was just finishing off a wall by laying a corner brick

Jim said to Mr Minns, 'Would you show me how to do that?' 'Not just at the moment, Jim, I'm busy,' said Mr Minns.

Jim left it for a few days and then gathering his courage he asked Mr Minns, 'Will you teach me how to lay bricks? I really want to have a go, Mr Minns.'

Mr Minns looked at Jim, not unkindly, 'There'll be time enough for that, Jim lad, time enough.' That evening, at supper with his parents, Jim looked downhearted. 'What's the matter, Jim?' asked his father. 'It's my work, Dad. I'm just not learning anything,' complained Jim. 'Well, Jim, have you told Mr Minns?' asked his father. 'Well, yes, Dad,' replied Jim. 'Well, Jim, it looks like you are going to have to ask him again,' replied his Dad. So the next day Jim did. Maybe he did not choose a good day, as Mr Minns was suffering from toothache that morning, but Jim was not to know that. 'Mr Minns, I want to learn to lay bricks, to build with them. When are you going to teach me?' Mr Minns took a deep breath, 'There'll be plenty of time for that, Jim,' he said somewhat irritably. 'Let's get this damn wall finished.' But Jim was persistent. 'Mr Minns, you agreed with my Dad that you would teach me to build and I'm just not learning. Are you going to teach me or not?'

This was too much for Mr Minns that morning: 'Now see here, Jim! If that's your attitude you aren't going to be learning from me. Maybe if you're not happy you'd better be looking for something else. Now let's have no more of your damn nonsense and let's get this bloody wall built.' Jim got on with mixing the mortar and carrying the bricks. He was not happy. What was he to do?

Exercise 4.6

1. How has Jim behaved in this situation?
2. How has Mr Minns behaved?
3. What is your advice to Jim?
4. Should Jim be looking for a new job?
5. If not, suggest assertive alternatives for Jim.

Now for our second example we shall look at a case where an employee has to deal with both a difficult customer and an unhelpful boss.

## Ruth, the shoe shop assistant

Ruth was a young woman employed in a shoe shop as a sales assistant. It was a small shop and very often Ruth was left on duty alone. The manager seemed to spend most of his time in the office at the back of the shop. One morning a customer came in; she was a large woman, middle-aged, and wearing an expensive fur coat. She was bearing aloft a pair of expensive 'fashion' boots that had been one of the shop's popular lines. She slammed them down on the counter. Ruth began to feel uncomfortable.

'Can I help you, Mrs Golding?' she asked. Ruth remembered Mrs Golding had returned goods before and had proved to be difficult.

'Yes, you certainly can! I should hope so. I'll have my money back on these. Quite unsatisfactory . . . unsatisfactory. . . .' Mrs Golding finished breathlessly.

Ruth examined the boots. They were badly scuffed and had obviously been worn for some time. One of the boots had a cut almost through the leather.

'Er . . . I'm sorry, Mrs Golding. How are they unsatisfactory?' Ruth asked. 'They just don't suit,' replied Mrs Golding. 'And they're worn.' Ruth examined the boots again. They had certainly been worn, but how long had Mrs Golding been wearing them?

'How long have you had them, Mrs Golding?' asked Ruth.

'Oh! I think I just bought them a few weeks ago. Anyway that doesn't matter. I'd just like my money back.'

Ruth was not quite sure what to do. Mrs Golding was a frequent customer and Ruth could not remember having sold her the boots. Ruth knew that if the boots were defective then it was the duty of the shop to refund Mrs Golding's money but she also knew that it wasn't up to the shop to provide Mrs Golding with replacement boots every time she wore a pair out.

'Excuse me, Mrs Golding,' Ruth said, 'I'll just have to speak to the manager about it.' Ruth left Mrs Golding in the shop and went into the manager's office. The manager, Mr Previn, glanced up from his order book. He was making up the accounts.

'I've got Mrs Golding in the shop, Mr Previn,' Ruth informed him. 'She's brought back a pair of boots. They're very worn and she's obviously had them some time. She wants her money back.'

'Well, she can't have it then!' snapped Mr Previn, annoyed at being disturbed. 'Tell her to go away.'

Ruth went back into the shop and confronted Mrs Golding. 'I've had a word with the manager and I'm sorry he says that we can't give you your money back. You've obviously worn the boots for some considerable time. They don't look like they've just suffered ordinary wear and tear.'

'Huh!' exploded Mrs Golding, 'I demand to see the manager.'

Ruth returned to Mr Previn. 'Just get rid of the old bat, Ruth,' he demanded.

Ruth went back into the shop unwillingly. 'I'm sorry, Mrs Golding, but the manager can't see you at the moment.'

Mrs Golding exploded. 'Very well then. You can keep your damn boots! I'm not coming here again!' She threw the boots on to the floor and stormed out, slamming the door behind her. Ruth felt upset. She felt she had done the right thing but had not got the right result. She had wanted Mr Previn's support and she had not got it.

Here is an exercise which may be used on an individual basis or for group discussion.

Exercise 4.7

1. Who in this story has been assertive, aggressive or passive?
2. How could any of them have behaved in more assertive ways?
3. How could Ruth get more support from her manager?
4. How can the shop deal assertively with Mrs Golding?

## ASSERTION AT YOUR WORK-PLACE

In your work, you will need to be aware of your achievements, otherwise you may lose out in pay and promotion. This loss can occur when the facts as to what you have, or have not, achieved emerge at your promotion reviews. These reviews may be formal, informal or even secret. In many organizations there is a review of each individual's progress each year. It is important that on going to your review you go equipped with the facts about your progress and achievements over the previous year. Do not leave this task to your manager. At the interview when the question is put, 'How do you feel you've done this last year?' or perhaps just, 'How do you feel you're getting on?' your response will be to give a brief summary of your achievements during the past year. This is the assertive approach. The passive answer, 'Oh, well, I think I'm getting on all right', is not going to impress anyone very much. Ask yourself, 'Would it impress you?'

The time to make any record of your achievements is as soon as possible afterwards. You will find it best to keep a running record of what you achieve. It is much easier than trying to remember afterwards, when you have to hand in your account at short notice. Your record of success should also make clear the difficulties you have overcome that are related to the work, as distinct from any personal problems you may have had. This is in phase with the basic concept that work is task orientated rather than personal/feeling orientated.

Exercise 4.8

1. In your work do you have formal job reviews?
2. Do you keep a record of your achievements?
3. Can you present these in an assertive way when the time comes?

Sometimes in a review or other situation an employee may be presented with such statements as 'We don't feel you're getting on very well' or 'We don't feel your attitude is what we need. You just don't fit the company image!' If challenged with criticisms of this form, and assuming that you still wish to work for the company, it is necessary for you to find out what is behind these rather vague statements. Then you may choose, or not, to alter whatever it is that is making your manager unhappy. If you do not get a straight answer it may be that your manager simply dislikes you. It happens. Or it could be that your manager is simply too embarrassed to tell you of any doubts that he or she may have. It would then be assertive for you to enquire as to what these are. When you know then you may be in a position to reassure your boss or perhaps to change your behaviour.

Exercise 4.9

1. What qualities do you think the managers of your firm expect from their employees?
2. How many of these attributes do you have?
3. As a manager are you clear which qualities you expect in members of your work-force?

4. As a manager how can you give honest information to your subordinates as to 'what is expected'?

In the absence of formal reviews, an employee who wants their worth recognized will often need to initiate the process. So suppose you are in a position where you are doing work which is at least as good as, or in fact better than, that of your colleagues who are on the same, or better, pay than you. What do you do about it? The passive attitude is nothing, and wait till your work is recognized. An aggressive attitude could lead to you picking a fight with your employer. This is seldom a good idea even if you are definitely leaving. The assertive response is to gather the facts about your progress and situation and then to present yourself and your case to your manager. The likely outcome of this assertive action is as follows.

The very least is that your initiative will be appreciated and the facts you present be placed on file in your manager's office (you have brought a spare copy for this purpose). You may get your rise or promotion or be put further up the list for when the next review is to be held. You may have the chance to attend courses or to undergo additional training. Perhaps your information is incorrect and your colleagues have duties or responsibilities of which you are not aware. Well, if that is the case, you will do your homework better next time. Perhaps, and this does happen sometimes, you will find that your firm is quite happy for you to do extra work without rewarding you. Indeed, they may even say so and that is the time when you will probably quietly, and without fuss, start looking for a firm where you will be paid properly for the work you do.

Exercise 4.10

1. Think of the best case you could make for extra pay or promotion.
2. Write it down and consider how realistic it is.
3. Rehearse presenting this case and perhaps engage a friend (not from work) to assist you in trying it out.

Sometimes an employer will undertake a formal job evaluation exercise and will employ an outside firm of management consultants for this task. They work with more exact ideas and formulae than your boss is likely to have available, which is of course why your firm has employed them. We shall now consider a story where this happens and some of the problems which may arise.

### Pauline's job evaluation

Pauline worked as an administrative assistant in an office concerned with the registration of shares. Her boss, John Quinn, had at first taken a great delight in showing Pauline how to do the work. He was not very keen on work himself and gradually Pauline took over most of his duties. John Quinn often signed Pauline's work before it left the office. So before long Pauline was doing most of the office work and it was at this time that the senior management of the company woke up to the fact that they did not know what was going on in general in their company. They decided to find out by employing a firm of job evaluation experts.

These experts duly arrived and presented Pauline with a form on which she was requested to write down the work she did. The form was required to be signed by Pauline's immediate manager, John Quinn, as is the usual practice in these job evaluations. Pauline completed her form honestly but with some trepidation, and brought it to John Quinn for his signature. Her anxiety was nothing compared with that of her boss as he read her form and was invited to counter-sign it.

'But look, Pauline,' he said, 'You've written down all these things. They're part of my job, my responsibility.'

'Well, yes,' replied Pauline, 'but the form did ask me to write down what I do and that's what I've done, just written it down.' John Quinn snorted. 'Well, I can't possibly sign this. It seems like I don't do anything.'

Pauline paused for a few moments wondering what to say. Then inspiration came. 'Well, you do have the overall responsibility and you do sign my work.' John Quinn was a worried man and he had had enough for the present. He yelled at Pauline, 'I'm not going to sign this. I'm not having you say you do all these things. It could cost me my job!' He took a red biro from his desk and crossed out several of the entries on Pauline's form and pushed it across his desk in her direction. 'Now go and sort it out!' he demanded.

Exercise 4.11

You are approached by the following people for your advice:

1. Pauline
2. John Quinn
3. Their senior manager

In each case how would you advise them, i.e. in what assertive ways could they behave in order to resolve the situation and support their legitimate interests adequately?

One of the problems that managers often experience occurs when the need arises to discipline or even to fire an employee. The subordinate is not likely to be very sympathetic under the circumstances and if you, as a manager, have a strong desire to be liked, then you are in trouble. The natural desire not to cause pain to your fellow humans is part of your humanity and is a feeling that it is necessary to accept rather than feel bad about. But there is a less noble feeling, that of being afraid of the employee's reaction on learning that he or she is about to be disciplined or fired. In either case, the first thing to do is to separate, as far as possible, the task orientation of work from the personal emotional need of being liked. If you can do this then it is possible to express sincere regret on a personal level, while still behaving in an assertive and efficient way.

Let us consider the situation where you as the person responsible have decided to fire an employee for a valid reason. We say, as the person responsible, because it seems to us that the person responsible for making serious decisions of this nature should have the responsibility of implementing them.

Exercise 4.12

You are the head of an old people's home. One of your care assistants has admitted stealing property from one of the residents. You know that the employee has been under considerable strain looking after their sick elderly father and has been very poorly off financially. Even so, your responsibility is to dismiss them.

1. How can you tell your employee in an assertive way that they are dismissed?

Now you are left with dealing with the emotional response of your employee. In fact, what you have to deal with is your own emotional reaction.

2. What do you anticipate the employee's reaction will be?
3. How can you respond assertively to this?

A final thought: being fired could be the best thing that happens to an employee, but maybe you should not count on the sacked person experiencing it in that way at the time.

Sometimes as an employee you will be in the position where a manager wants to fire you, but lacks the power. Such situations occur frequently in the public sectors. For example in the case of a lecturer in Further Education, the manager is the head of department but the right to hire and fire belongs to the Local Education Committee. This division of responsibility is unfortunate as both employee and manager may be stuck in a situation which suits neither of them. Let us consider the case of Paul.

### Paul's problem

Paul was a man of 30 who had spent the first part of his working life as a technician in industry. When he was made redundant he was 'lucky' in finding a post teaching at his local technical college. He enjoyed teaching and the contact with his students and colleagues. Unfortunately Paul experienced difficulties in his personal life. The stress of being made redundant, a short period of unemployment and his new job proved too much for his wife and their marriage. She petitioned for divorce and to this Paul responded with anger and depression. This depression affected his performance at work. Paul was responsible for examining his students and some of his marking was so erratic that his colleagues had to re-mark some of his work. They were sympathetic with Paul on a personal level, but that is only one of the ways they related to Paul.

Paul's manager took a much stronger line. He had been very keen on employing Paul for the post and was furious that Paul was not living up to his expectations. Paul was absent from work while he was sick. When he returned, he was interviewed by his manager.

'Hello, Paul. I'm sorry you've been ill and that things haven't worked out here. I'm going to have to let you go. I'm sorry but there it is,' Paul's manager finished lamely.

Paul felt very angry; 'You can't do that!' he stormed. 'Anyway you don't have the power to sack me. Only the Education Committee can do that. I've been ill. I'm going to report you to the Union.'

The manager had only recently joined the Union and he knew that Paul was right in that he could not in fact sack Paul. But he had chosen Paul for the job and Paul had let him down. He glared at Paul and said as threateningly as he could manage, 'I'll make damn sure you won't be working here any more!' and with that the interview ended.

Paul subsequently found that his timetable for the next year consisted entirely of low-level work which gave him little opportunity to use his skills, but he did this work well and his students gained good results. At the end of the year his manager said, 'Well, you seem to be getting on now' and that was that. Paul did not enquire further and left matters for another year when again his students gained good results. This time he determined to resolve the matter with his manager. He confronted his manager.

'My students have good results again. That's for two years now. I know I was depressed and didn't work properly but I'm fine now and anyway that was over two years ago. I'd like you to give me some higher-level work this year.'

Paul's manager was not in a good mood at the time. 'No,' he snapped, 'I told you two years ago that I was getting rid of you and that's exactly what I'm going to do.'

'But you can't do that!' responded Paul angrily. 'Just you wait and see!' replied his manager.

Exercise 4.13

1. How have Paul and his manager behaved?
2. How could each of them have behaved in more assertive ways?
3. What is each of them to do now?

## NEW WORK-STYLES

Nowadays work patterns are altering for many people. These include an increase in part-time and flexi-time work as well as self-employment in self-created work patterns. People following such work-styles need to behave assertively in such matters as organizing their time, charging adequately for their services, and ensuring that they have sufficient leisure time. These new ways of organizing one's work are often experienced as very rewarding and creative to these new workers.

# Chapter Five

# USING ANGER CREATIVELY

How do you feel about anger? How do you feel about feeling angry? Do you deny it? Do you suppress it? Do you express it, regardless of whether it is in your best interests to do so? Or do you, perhaps, simply accept it, along with all the other emotions you experience?

It is quite normal to feel angry or irritated or frustrated. It is difficult to be human and live in the world without feeling these emotions sometimes. The emotion of anger tends to be a particularly strong one, and it is important to take a look at how anger operates in our lives. If we know more about it, then we can take steps towards dealing with it productively and assertively.

Let us look at how people feel about anger. Most of us find anger difficult to deal with because we experience it as a very strong emotion. In western societies in particular expressing emotions is not very acceptable, so we tend to feel guilty and uncomfortable about expressing them at all – especially anger, which seems so unwieldy. Often we deny even feeling angry. It seems easier, sometimes, than coping with the hassle of working out what to do with it. But is it really easier in the end? Have you ever suppressed or denied your anger at the time of feeling it, only to have it erupt inappropriately in a completely different situation? We are not saying it is always appropriate to express anger, but as with other feelings, it is always a good idea to tell yourself the truth about what you are feeling, to acknowledge it. It is only from a point of truth within yourself that you can act creatively and really constructively in your life.

## WHY DO WE GET ANGRY?

Broadly the times when we get angry can be categorized as follows.

1. When we feel thwarted, threatened or disrespected in some way; when the path towards our chosen goals has seemingly been blocked by someone else's action.
2. As a defence, when really we are desperately hurt, but do not want to appear vulnerable, so we show anger instead.
3. When a situation or action by someone else has triggered off memories of an unfinished situation in our past.
4. When we feel our rights have been violated, or someone has 'done us wrong'.
5. When we are frightened or feeling inadequate in some way, and feel angry with ourselves.

### Angry feelings

We do feel angry sometimes, but few of us know what to do with these feelings. To understand why this is so, and in order to explore where anger comes from, let us look briefly at some of the feelings which may accompany anger.

### Self-righteousness

When we are angry about something we tend to believe ourselves to be in the right – and the other person wrong. A question to ask yourself in these circumstances is – is that true? If we have believed this and then choose to say we are angry, it is likely to emerge in an aggressive and accusatory manner. Ask yourself, do you want to punish the other person?

### Indignation

The 'How dare they?' syndrome. If you experience even a smattering of this feeling, it could be that you are taking yourself too seriously or taking what someone does far more personally than is good for you. For example, if a friend has promised to telephone by Monday to tell you whether she will be able to help with the party, and it is now Wednesday, and she still has not telephoned – if this makes you feel angry and indignant, stop to consider whether it may be other things going on in her life that have prevented her from telephoning, rather than that she has no respect for you. This will not make the anger go away, but it will put it in perspective.

## Low self-esteem

Much has been said about this, and ways of dealing with it. The truth is that if we feel badly about ourselves, we are more likely to take things personally, to regard someone's action as a personal attack or insult, when that was not intended.

## Judging

This is closely linked with the previous three and particularly with self-righteousness. Someone has done something that we do not agree with and therefore 'she must be wrong'. This is the way the thinking tends to go if you are being judgemental: 'he must be pretty stupid anyway', and so on.

What tends to happen if we have any of these thoughts and feelings, of course, is that they come out when we speak to the individuals concerned. Few people are able to express angry feelings clearly and directly.

### *Is anger useful? How?*

## Positive action

It is a reminder that all is not as we want it to be in our world. Dissatisfaction is a positive thing. Without it, we would simply put up with life as it is and not take any action to further our goals. For example if women early this century had not felt angry at their disenfranchisement, they would not have fought for the vote.

## Releasing stress

Expressing anger can be a great stress-releaser: feelings which might otherwise get suppressed and cause distress or even illness may be released. This does not mean it is necessary to express it to the person we think we feel angry with.

## Increased openness

It can lead to increased openness in relationships and an increased trust. There is a feeling of respect engendered if you know someone is willing to talk to you about the more difficult areas, not just skim over them as if they did not exist.

## Unblocking feelings

If we are in touch with our feelings, including anger, as they occur, and deal with them appropriately, we then stand less chance of creating a backlog of unexpressed or blocked feelings which can lead to internal stress and serious miscommunication.

## Achieving objectives

Importantly, the energy contained in the emotion of anger has the same quality as that which pushes us to do things to further our goals. Used correctly, it can assist us in being assertive and expressing ourselves and going for what we want in life. But it must be carefully handled.

### Anger can be a very destructive emotion

1. Anger can lead to bad power conflicts, with both parties maintaining the rightness of their viewpoints.
2. When expressing anger, it is easy to trigger past unresolved or unexpressed anger, and thus 'go over the top'.
3. Following from the above, the recipient may misunderstand and there may be confusion.
4. Anger can lead to irrational or confused thought. We can become obsessed at 'righting the wrong' that has been done to us and focus out-of-proportionately on the past injustice rather than on the present.

### Some of the signs of hidden anger

It is assertive to acknowledge anger – or any other feeling, if you are experiencing it. But sometimes you do not actually realize that what you are feeling is anger. You know there is 'something wrong', but cannot pinpoint what it is. These are some of the signs:

1. Overeating, drinking too much or inexplicable body pains can be signs that you are angry, and turning the anger in on yourself.

2. Anger may well be operating if you find yourself getting irritated easily, for example when driving or going about ordinary daily activity; if you are finding any excuse to create a conflict; or rather than telling someone something in a direct manner, you get your own back in subtle ways.
3. If you find you are blaming other people a lot, or feeling you must get away from it all, or feeling hurt or victimized, you may in fact be feeling angry about something quite unconnected with that situation.
4. Internalized anger can, in fact, lead to (severe) depression. Ignoring the fact that you are feeling angry can quite literally make you ill.

### About your anger

There are some other things that are useful to know about your own anger which will help you to decide how to deal with it.

First, how was anger dealt with in your childhood environment? Were you frightened by it? Were you excited? Was it expressed or suppressed? What was your reaction to that? Were you encouraged to express anger or not?

If you were not allowed to express anger as a child, or if your anger was not acknowledged, then you may not be aware of occasions when you get angry now; we have spoken of clues to watch for in order to know when you are actually angry. If yours was a family where your reactions were very strictly monitored, any anger you may feel now may be at an unconscious level, and liable to erupt without warning.

Alternatively you may have been allowed to have your own way too much as a child; perhaps you did not have sufficient guidance and discipline. In this case you may still act like a child if your desires are thwarted, and become angry and/or sulky. In this case, you can ask yourself if such behaviour serves the adult you are now.

Second, do you generally feel hard done by in your life? Do you feel fairly powerless and often a victim? Do you feel you often do not get your needs met? This is not anger which needs to be expressed to a particular person; more, it is a frustration with your particular situation in life. If you take the step of acknowledging that you are responsible for your situation, you stand more chance of being able to change it.

For example you might not be getting enough enjoyment in your life: make an agreement with yourself to do more things you enjoy doing. You might not be feeling stretched enough: take more risks. You may not be feeling appreciated: be more appreciative of yourself. That is where it all must begin – with you.

Take a look and see what is causing your irritation or anger, and see if you can take steps towards doing what is necessary to help you to feel more fulfilled in that area of your life. The energy contained in anger is the same energy that we use to be assertive in our lives, to fulfil ourselves. The more we can channel anger to this end, the less likely we are to waste it on minor frustrations and irritations.

Third, do you have past, unresolved anger lurking in your psyche? If so, certain situations or happenings are likely to trigger this, and cause you to overreact. Get to know your own trigger points. It may be that you become angry easily with a particular person or type of person. If you become aware in this way of your patterns of reaction, you are going to be more in charge of your anger and how to deal with it.

Perhaps you have now become clearer about when your anger is likely to be triggered and why, and what your patterns of action are.

What can you do about expressing anger? Is it a good idea to do so or not? The answer is sometimes yes, and sometimes no.

## WHEN TO EXPRESS ANGER

There are keys as to whether it is wise to express anger at a particular time or not.

First, find out what your goal is in the situation. Would it best serve your purpose if you expressed your anger or not? For example if you are angry with someone for not doing something which he or she had promised to do, expressing your anger may not be the best way of encouraging the person to do it the next time. It might be more effective to focus on your goal in the situation, rather than on your (albeit understandable) feelings of frustration, and say something like, 'I'd really appreciate it if next time you'd shut the door.' Explain it from your point of view and what it would mean for you.

It is worth remembering that even when you express anger in

a straightforward and non-accusatory manner, people are inclined to feel criticized and become defensive. It is worth taking this into account, and making it clear that you are not getting at them, but simply being honest about what you are feeling.

Second, do you want to blame or accuse, or do you genuinely want to clarify the situation? Be honest with yourself here; it is easy to deceive yourself about your motives. Be particularly careful if you are dealing with someone with whom you have a close relationship. Here especially it is easy to bring in anger from the past. The other person will feel overwhelmed or unfairly treated; you will probably feel guilty for having gone 'over the top'; rather than clarification, you will have reached a point of more confusion and hostility.

Third, it could be that you are using expressing anger to a particular individual as an outlet for anger you feel generally about your situation in life, or for anger you feel towards someone else. This obviously achieves nothing – except perhaps a temporary relief. But it also causes further aggravation between you and the recipient.

Finally, closely connected with the above is acting on the dangerous belief 'The world owes me.' This is about having an inbuilt demand that things go your way, and being absolutely furious when this does not happen. Examples of messages of this nature which you might be giving yourself are:

'People should know what I want without me having to ask.
– I shouldn't have to wait.
– I shouldn't have to do housework.
– I shouldn't have to hang around in this traffic jam.
– I shouldn't have to earn enough money to live on.'

Here you are not being honest with yourself about what is happening in your life. You are blaming the world in general for your situation. If there are lots of these kinds of messages in your head, you are probably feeling like a victim in many areas of your life. Such messages are perhaps a desperate and illogical attempt to feel in control of your life. Examining beliefs and self-talk can be very empowering; it can enable you to move from victim to person in charge of creating his or her life. It is a lot more constructive than dumping your anger on someone else.

Exercise 5.1 (see Notes, p. 131)

If you find you are giving yourself a negative message

1. Stop.
2. Ask yourself, is telling myself this useful to me, does it help me to get where I want to go in my life?
3. If it is not useful, what would be an alternative, more constructive, message?
4. Try substituting this for the original message.

This takes practice, but is well worth doing.

Exercise 5.2 (see Notes, p. 132)

1. Think about what obligations you have towards other people, things you feel you owe them. These could be material things or actions (for example a visit every month), or less concrete like love.
2. Think about what you owe yourself.
3. Think about what you imagine people owe you, what obligations you feel they have towards you.
4. Ask yourself if this is true – do you really owe these people, do they owe you?
5. Ask yourself if having these ties and restrictions is of benefit to you in your life.
6. See if you can let go of any of them; see if you can take the 'ought' out of these situations, and do these things if you choose to and have other people do only if they choose to.
7. Notice if you feel freer now that you no longer have these ties. Notice how much more you are able to live in the present.

*Expressing anger directly to the person concerned*

This may be appropriate

1. When you have a conflict, misunderstanding or miscommunication with someone which you genuinely want to work through. When you feel love, liking and respect for the other person and are willing to listen to his or her point of view.
2. When you are in touch with your wider goals and choices and

not obsessed with getting your own back or explaining your point of view repeatedly.

3. When you are willing to be open and perhaps make yourself vulnerable to the person, rather than pretend you have not been affected by something the person said.

4. When the other person's action has affected yourself and other people. For example in a work situation where one person's failure to complete a task has far-reaching effects; here it would be important to inform the person of the effect their action has had, in order that they do not repeat it.

5. The key to dealing with angry feelings constructively, as with expressing other feelings, is to own them for yourself, and simply make a statement about them to the other person.

### Other ways of dealing with anger

First, you could tell a friend how angry you are about something that has happened. Part of being assertive is being open and honest about your feelings – saying what is going on, rather than just 'Oh, I'm fine'. It is possible to do this in a way that simply reports it. It is not necessary to wallow in the feelings.

Second, if you are feeling very angry about something and it is making you feel tense and anxious and miserable, you could choose to let go of it instead of focusing on it and giving it energy. You may think this is not as simple as it sounds. It certainly is not impossible.

Third, you could do relaxation exercises as a way of focusing on something different from your anger; as you learn to relax, your ability to choose what you want and not react to circumstances increases. Or you could listen to soothing music.

Fourth, physical exercise is a good channel for angry feelings; different things suit different people. Making sure you get enough exercise generally is wise, and helps you to feel relaxed in body and mind.

Finally, respond in a different way. An aid to this is giving people the benefit of the doubt. For example if you think someone is behaving in an insulting way towards you, you are likely to be angry. If instead you simply assume they were being thoughtless, you are more likely to shrug it off or forget about it.

Many of us feel that struggling is a necessary component of

living in the world and because we are used to giving ourselves hard times, we tend to focus on negative things and not let go. At such times, think about what you want for yourself; ask yourself do you really want to be tense and anxious? Begin to notice what else is happening, what else you could focus on.

For example June was feeling very irritated with a colleague who had been rude to her at work. She was new there and had not felt able to tell the other woman how she felt; she had brought her irritation home with her. That morning, she had received two items in the post which had pleased her. One was a lovely postcard from a friend on holiday in Greece. June had felt happy to know she was being thought of. The other was a letter inviting her to the country for the weekend. At lunchtime, she had been shopping and found just what she wanted for a friend's birthday, which had pleased her. Now she had forgotten all about these things, as her anger took pride of place in her thoughts.

June decided to take responsibility for doing something about it. 'Do I want to feel like this – tense and unrelaxed?' The answer was no. 'What could I do about it?'

First, she telephoned a friend and spoke about the incident with the woman at work. Her friend listened and commented, and June felt relieved. Next, she sat down and reviewed her day, and remembered the mail and the shopping at lunchtime. She made a conscious choice to stop focusing on her anger and to focus instead on her feelings of pleasure and of appreciation. She became more relaxed.

Your reality is dictated by what you think is true, and the messages you give yourself. You could choose to laugh at a situation, rather than make a 'big deal' of it.

### Guidelines for expressing anger

1. Be clear and specific and take responsibility for your statement. Don't blame. For example 'I feel angry when you're late!', not 'You make me feel angry.'
2. Listen to the other person's point of view.
3. Focus on your goal of getting your statement across clearly, and don't get stuck with negative feelings.
4. Sometimes we express our anger, but hold on to some of it, perhaps, because we are afraid of really being honest about

showing it. The assertive approach is acknowledging that you have the right to express your feelings. Do not smile when you are saying you are angry. If you do, what will come across is the mixed message that you do not really mean what you are saying.

5. It is possible to express anger and show you care about the person at the same time. For example 'I realize you may find this difficult to understand, I realize you were in a hurry, but I didn't like the way you cut me short this morning.'

### Further exercises on anger

Exercise 5.3 (see Notes, p. 132)

1. Think of a time in your life when you felt angry about something. What was it?
2. What feelings accompanied the feelings of anger? Take a longer look at the feelings. Would it have been useful to express them?
3. If not, would any other action have been useful in the circumstances? For example if an accompanying feeling is low self-esteem, you might want to say some affirmations to yourself. If an accompanying feeling is indignation, you might want to ask yourself what you genuinely think the other person's intention was in taking the action that affected you. Very likely, they did not mean to disturb you, and you are taking it too personally.

Separating out our feelings in this way helps us to realize that we are in charge of them and that we can choose what we do with our feelings.

Exercise 5.4

If you feel very indignant or self-righteous about something, take the opportunity to look at why you are reacting so strongly. Often we strongly criticize other people for things we in fact do ourselves. So next time you feel this way, take a look at your behaviour and you might even find yourself having a little chuckle to yourself as you realize you were being judgemental towards somebody about something you do yourself!

Exercise 5.5 (see Notes, p. 133)

1. Think of a time when you were angry and did not acknowledge it to yourself – pretended that you were not – and the anger came out anyway, but inappropriately.
2. What happened?
3. Who did you express it to, and what were the consequences?
4. If you could re-play the incident, how would you do it differently?

Exercise 5.6

Exploring your anger. Complete the following statements:
1. When someone expresses anger towards me, I . . .
2. When I feel angry with a friend, I . . .
3. When I feel angry with someone I'm close to, I . . .
4. When I feel angry with an acquaintance or in a social or work situation, I . . .
5. If I express my anger, I feel . . .
6. If I suppress my anger, I feel . . .
7. Three situations that would undoubtedly make me angry are . . .
8. If I express my anger, what happens is . . .
9. A time when I expressed my anger and felt complete . . .

Exercise 5.7

1. How do you think your anger comes out?
   Of the following, which do you think may act as vehicles for your unexpressed anger:
   – Overeating
   – Overdrinking
   – Making barbed jokes
   – Using drugs
   – Body pains
   – Depression
   – Sabotaging
   – Feeling guilty
   – Blaming
   – Being a victim
   – Sadness
   – A feeling of wanting to get away from it all.

2. Next time you feel this is happening, as a first step, acknowledge to yourself that you are angry.
3. Ask yourself how it would be appropriate to deal with it:
   - What do you want to achieve?
   - Read through 'When to express anger' (p. 50); are you doing any of these?
   - Is it a good idea to express it to the person or to deal with it in another way?
4. Make a choice to deal with it. Choose whichever are appropriate:
   - Acknowledging it
   - Speaking to someone about it
   - Letting go
   - Sublimating it through another chosen activity
   - Focusing on something else
   - Expressing it to the person concerned.

# Chapter Six

# MAKING REQUESTS – SAYING 'YES' AND SAYING 'NO'

## MAKING REQUESTS

When we make a request we give another person an opportunity to give us what we ask for. Sadly many of us find making requests difficult, but we can learn how to ask for what we want assertively. Why may it be difficult to ask? The answers come from our history and our present experience.

### *Our history*

In our childhood, we unselfconsciously demanded what we wanted when we wanted it. We needed our parents to say 'no' in order to create a bounded secure environment for us. But we did therefore have repeated experiences of our requests being rejected. Often these rejections became emotionally charged as we learned that repeatedly making demands was an easy way to annoy and provoke our parents. We also needed our parents to say 'yes' when appropriate and to praise and encourage us. Not all of us had as much of these positive experiences as we needed.

As we grew up, most of us have learned, more or less, to make requests which are reasonable and appropriate. We became more discerning as to when, how and who to ask as we made requests to our peers and others. If we thought well of ourselves, then we would find it easy to make requests but, if not, then making even the most reasonable requests would be experienced as stress-producing and difficult. If our request was refused, we experienced ourselves as being rejected and felt perhaps: 'I'm not worth it', 'I'm not really entitled to it.' Thus our self-esteem was undermined. Nobody is fully confident in everything, but we can learn to use assertive techniques to give us the best chance of getting what we want. Whether or not we succeed in this, we will increase our self-esteem by trying.

## Present experience

Let us consider our present. For example, 'I'd like to ask her or him for this or that. But I can't! Why can't I?' The reasons we may come up with may be:

1. They might say 'No': I might fail to get what I want.
2. They might say 'Yes': do I really want it after all?
3. I might feel rejected if they refuse my request.
4. They might think badly of me for asking this of them.
5. If I ask, they will think that I cannot cope.
6. If I ask, I will make myself vulnerable.

Here is an exercise to enable you to find out how you may feel about making requests.

Exercise 6.1

1. When you are tempted not to ask, do you give yourself similar reasons to the above?
2. What other reasons do you give yourself for not asking for what you want?
3. Ask yourself the following questions about these reasons:
   – Is what you are telling yourself likely to be true?
   – How much does it matter to you?

Now let us look at some of the possibilities.

They might say 'No': I might fail to get what I want

Yes, of course this might happen. We all have the right to say no. You may feel disappointed that you have not got what you want. What else do you feel? When we ask people this, the most common response is 'I feel I've failed'. Now this statement is ambiguous. You have indeed failed, at least for the present, to obtain what you want, but that is all. You have behaved assertively in asking and giving yourself your best chance of succeeding. In this aspect you have succeeded, not failed. Fear of failure is one of the commonest reasons for not asking. It depends on what you choose 'failure' to mean.

### They might say 'Yes': do I really want it after all?

The question to ask yourself is: 'Do I really want what I am asking for?' This is a very important question and it is unhelpful to mix it up with the different questions, 'Will I get it?' or 'Am I worth it?' The best idea is to make up your mind about what it is you want first. You may not be absolutely certain what it is you want, but at least be clear what it is you are asking. Do not pretend that you really want whatever the other person chooses to give you. Is it so dreadful to succeed both in being assertive and in getting what you want? The answer to this may be 'yes' if you fear success. This fear of success is much more common than may be realized in our success-orientated culture. It is important to define what success means to you. For example if success means taking action to support being true to yourself, then it will be important to ask if you want to ask.

### I might feel rejected if they refuse my request

It is important to distinguish between being rejected as a person and having your request rejected. Many of us feel rejected easily because of negative childhood experiences. You have the right to ask. You do not have the right to expect the other person to say yes.

### They might think badly of me for asking this of them

They might. But it is important to be in touch with your own assessment of yourself, rather than emphasizing someone else's opinion of you, which, in fact, probably says more about them than about you. If someone, for example your boss, has the power to give you what you want, clearly his or her opinion is important, as this will influence whether or not you get it. However, you can still aim to make an accurate self-assessment – is it more important to ask, or is it more important to have someone else's approval?

### If I ask, they will think that I cannot cope

Well, maybe you do have more to do than you can handle at that particular time. That is not terrible. It is important to acknowledge when we need help. Often people feel very happy to be asked.

## If I ask, I will make myself vulnerable, perhaps powerless

You make yourself vulnerable by asking only if you are dependent on the person to reply in one particular way. Under certain circumstances you are in fact very dependent on another person. If you are lost in the desert and dying of thirst then you would be dependent on your friend who has a full water bottle. Most of our life does not involve such extreme physical dependence; our emotional dependence is something we can learn to change.

Now let us to consider the possible responses to our requests and the possible responses we might make to the requests from others.

## SAYING 'YES' AND SAYING 'NO'

Saying 'Yes' and saying 'No' are important responses which an assertive person needs to be able to make. They are important ways we have of defining ourselves and showing other people how we wish to be treated and where our boundaries are. They are not the only assertive responses that we may wish to make in a particular situation. But why is it so important to be able to say 'No'? In the first instance let us consider the example in the following section.

### Susan's lunch break

Susan had worked as an administrative assistant in Social Services for two months. She was one of two administrative assistants in that particular section. She worked hard and enjoyed her job. The only thing that bothered Susan about the work was that sometimes Linda, the other administrative assistant, palmed work off on to Susan which, it seemed to Susan, she could have done herself. The trouble was that the division of work was not completely clear. Both of them worked for four social workers; typing was given to whoever had the lowest pile of work at that moment.

One day, Susan had worked through her lunch-hour, taking

time only to nibble a roll at her desk. She still had a pile of typing in her in-tray, and also some filing to do. She was just taking stock, and deciding how much she could realistically accomplish during the remainder of the day, when Linda came over to her desk. 'Be a love, Sue,' she said. 'I'm up to my ears, and Malcolm must have this chart typed by the end of the afternoon. Would you be an angel, and do it?'

Susan felt tense, resentful and put-upon. It was obvious that she had at least as much work as the other woman. But if she said 'No', Linda would think she couldn't cope. 'Oh, all right,' she said. 'Leave it there.'

Now what is happening? Susan feels like a victim. She is not taking responsibility for getting her needs met. She is allowing the situation, the fact that Linda has been there longer than her, to get her down. She is not really giving any credence to what she wants, what would be good for her.

One specific action which Susan could have taken to ameliorate the situation would have been to clarify the division of work. She could have also given herself positive messages in the situation. This is what we have to say about the situation. What do you say?

Susan's story as we have recorded it is fairly straightforward. We now move to a more complex set of circumstances in 'Evening off'.

### Evening off

Mary O'Donnell was a student nurse in her third and final year of training at a London teaching hospital. She had come over from Ireland just over two years ago from a large family in a small farming community. Mary was one of four students on the orthopaedic ward. She enjoyed the work and had done well in her previous year's nursing exams. However, the nursing officer in charge of the ward, Sister Wood, seemed to have taken a dislike to Student Nurse O'Donnell. Mary always seemed to be given the unpleasant jobs, of which there were plenty. Also there was plenty of overtime, usually unpaid, and Mary normally did more than her share. Mary's sister, Bernadette, was coming over on Tuesday on her way from Germany and Mary had arranged to meet her at the airport.

On the Monday afternoon Sister Wood walked briskly behind the screens where Mary was attending to Mr Morris. Mr Morris had his leg in a plaster cast and was not wholly happy with life. As Sister Wood entered he jumped with surprise and startled, winced in pain.

'Be careful, nurse,' snapped Sister Wood.

'Sorry, are you all right, Mr Morris?' asked Mary anxiously.

'I'm sure you're all right. Aren't you, Mr Morris?' enquired Sister Wood sharply.

Mr Morris did not feel at all 'all right', but felt it would be unwise to say so and gave what, he hoped, was an appropriately grateful smile.

'Yes. Thank you, Sister. I'm doing fine.'

'A word with you, Student Nurse O'Donnell,' said Sister sharply.

Mary moved to the end of the bed, where Sister Wood looked her straight in the eyes. Mary avoided her gaze and looked downward.

'Nothing important on tomorrow, Mary, I hope?' Sister Wood stated rather than asked, and continued without waiting for a reply. 'I need you on duty tomorrow evening. Student Nurse Fenton is sick again.'

Mary, still looking at the floor, said in a small voice, 'I'm sorry, Sister; I'm meeting my sister tomorrow evening.'

'No, nurse,' began Sister Wood firmly and almost kindly. 'In this work we often have to give up our social activities for the sake of our patients. I'm sure you understand that and I'm sure you want to be a good and responsible nurse. So I'm sure that if you think about it you will be able to meet your sister some other time. Isn't that so?'

'Well . . . er . . . yes. I suppose so, Sister,' murmured Mary, her eyes scarcely moving from the end of the bed.

'Good girl. I knew I could rely on you,' replied Sister Wood with satisfaction.

Let us look at what is happening in this story. Here is an exercise.

Exercise 6.2

1. How do you think Mary is behaving? What messages is she giving herself and what are the consequences of her behaviour? For instance what is Mary going to tell her sister Bernadette?

2. Do you think that Sister Wood was behaving fairly towards Mary and do you think that 'being a good and responsible nurse' means giving up social engagements? Do student nurses have to behave only in passive and obedient ways?
3. Suppose you were a friend of Mary's, what would your advice be to her, i.e. how do you think that she could change the messages she is giving herself, and consequently her behaviour, so that she can have more of what she wants? What could she have said to Sister Wood and how could she have said it?

In fairness to Mary it is possible that however assertive she is she will have continuing trouble with Sister Wood. We remind you that we do not claim assertive behaviour to be the answer to every problem. But we do say that Mary will need to behave assertively as well as whatever other steps she needs to take. What do you think these might be?

Finally let us consider another case which illustrates how 'saying no' is an important professional skill. Here a doctor needs to say no to a patient's request in order to do her work properly.

### Can I have the orange tablets?

Dr Lambert was in the surgery fifteen minutes early as usual. She was new to the job and keen. Dr Brown was late as usual but Dr Merry was there.

'Good morning, Dr Lambert,' said Dr Merry.

'Good morning, Dr Merry,' said Dr Lambert.

They had greeted each other in this way for the two months she had been working with the practice and it had now become a ritual. They looked at the files of the patients they were going to see that morning.

'Got anything interesting, Ann?' asked Dr Merry.

'Well, yes, there's Bill Frances. I haven't seen him before. Do you know anything about him, Dave?'

'Now, Ann,' began Dr Merry, settling himself down as though they had all day. 'Let me tell you about Bill Frances. He's an engineer down at the Ford Works. Used to be good money and secure. Not so sure of that nowadays. Anyway he's married, two kids. His wife is often in here, generally minor things: colds, flu, bit of digestive trouble, headaches, you know the sort of thing. Now then, whatever his wife has, Bill Frances is in the next week and he's got it too. Regular as clockwork.'

'Mumm . . . sympathetic symptoms,' murmured Dr Lambert.

Mr Frances walked into the consulting room and sat down, hesitating slightly. 'Good morning, Mr Frances,' said Dr Lambert. Mr Frances looked uneasy. 'Morning, love, I usually see Dr Merry or Dr Brown.'

Ann Lambert had heard this many times over the last two months, sometimes accompanied by 'You're very young, aren't you?' from the older and less inhibited patients. She had evolved a way of dealing with the situation.

'That's quite all right, Mr Frances. I'm working with Dr Brown and Dr Merry. How can I help you?' Dr Lambert said firmly and with a confidence she was just beginning to get used to.

'Well, er . . . um . . . Doctor,' began Mr Frances. Then finally deciding to accept Dr Lambert as a real doctor, 'I've got bronchitis and I need some of those orange pills, amfo . . . something or other.'

'Ampicillin?' asked Dr Lambert.

'Yes, that's it. Amfocillin, love,' replied Mr Frances.

'Well, why do you think you've got bronchitis?' enquired Dr Lambert.

'My wife's been ill with it for the last two weeks,' replied Mr Frances, 'and I've caught it from her.'

'How is she? Getting better?' asked Dr Lambert.

'Oh, yes. She's all right, love. I've got it now.'

'Would you just lie down on the couch and let me have a look at you?' instructed Dr Lambert.

Three minutes later Dr Lambert was convinced that Mr Frances was suffering from influenza, not bronchitis.

'You've got the flu,' said Dr Lambert. 'Go to bed for a few days, keep warm, plenty to drink and a few aspirins should see you right.'

Mr Frances looked unhappy. 'I'd still like some of the orange tablets, the amfocillin. Can I have some?'

'No,' said Dr Lambert. 'You don't need them. Influenza is caused by a virus and antibiotics don't work on viruses.'

'Oh!' said Mr Frances. 'I'm sure Dr Merry would have given me some.'

'I don't think so,' replied Dr Lambert quietly. 'Don't worry; you'll be quite well soon,'

'Well, I hope so, love,' muttered Mr Frances doubtfully.

'Good morning, then,' said Dr Lambert.

'Good morning, love,' said Mr Frances.

'Oh! Just one more thing, Mr Frances. Please don't call me "love". My name is Ann Lambert and I'd be happy for you to call me that, or Doctor.'

Mr Frances left the consulting room. Seeing the doctor had not been at all what he had expected.

The stereotype of a doctor as a middle-aged man dies hard. If you are a doctor who is young, female (particularly a pretty female) or possibly not white-British then you may have a problem being recognized as a professionally competent person. Other myths die equally hard: for instance, the myth that you go to the doctor when you are ill; 'he' gives you a prescription for medicine which you take and get better; the doctor has cured you. Many patients find it hard to believe that many minor illnesses get better without medicine, some even without doctors. Prescribing drugs such as antibiotics for their placebo effect has been the practice with some doctors who take the attitude that: it works; my patient has got better; that's my job done. However, Dr Lambert is not one of these. She has clearly established how she wants to be treated.

Exercise 6.3

1. How has Dr Lambert established the way in which she wants to be treated?
2. Do you think that Mr Frances will have confidence in her medical judgement?
3. Do you think that accepting being called by her first name might lessen her authority?
4. Would you call your doctor by his or her first name?
5. If not, but your doctor addresses you by your first name, why is that? How do you feel about it, and what could you do about it?

Note: Dr Lambert does not challenge Mr Frances directly. She does not say 'You are wrong' but she does state clearly and assertively what her diagnosis is and how she expects to be treated.

*Why say 'No'?*

Probably by this time we have given you a very clear idea about the need to be able to say no and we hope we have stimulated thought about other situations including ones in which you are involved, where being able to say no would be useful to you. Not saying no when you want to means that you are placing more importance on the other person's needs than on your own. You are failing to draw boundaries. It can create future problems and we think that it is far better to be honest in the first instance. Would you prefer it if someone said no to you when that was what they meant rather than said yes? Would you prefer them to be honest with you? When learning to say no, it can be useful to identify what it is that you are afraid may happen or what you think the other person will think of you if you say no.

*Why is it difficult to say 'No'?*

What stops you from saying no in any particular situation? Let us look at some of the major reasons.

If I say no, they may feel hurt or rejected

This, of course, is possible. If you say no to a particular request, the other person may feel rejected as a person. But you cannot be responsible for someone else's feelings; you can be responsible only for yourself. If you know this person feels easily rejected, you can say, 'I don't want you to feel bad or rejected, but . . .' and then add your statement. This shows that you are taking this person's feelings into account – but not holding yourself responsible for them. It is patronizing to think we can be in charge of other people's feelings.

If I say no this time, they may not like me any more

Ask yourself – is this really likely? And if it is, do you really want such a person as a friend anyway, if they do not respect your right to say no?

If I say no this time, they may never ask again

This, too, is possible – but irrelevant. You can deal only with one situation at a time. You cannot control how someone else is going to act in the future. Besides it is always possible to say 'Do ask me another time' to make it clear you are saying no then, but not necessarily for always.

### They won't take any notice if I say no

You do not absolutely know this, although your past experience with this person may tell you that this is very likely. Even if they do not, at least you will have taken the step of setting your boundaries. So you will have succeeded in the first stage of being assertive.

### They'd say yes to me (and so I'll feel guilty if I refuse them)

This is another instance of getting two situations confused. What you do is your responsibility; what they do is theirs. Feeling guilty is largely a habit and, to our knowledge, no good ever came of it. As you practise being assertive, the guilty feelings will lessen over time.

### I can't say no, because I feel sorry for them

'If I say no, perhaps no one else will be able or willing to help them out, and so, they will be stuck.' If you need to say no for whatever reason, for example other commitments you have, saying yes and putting yourself under pressure will only make you feel angry with yourself and resentful towards the other person. At worst, it may mar the friendship.

Do not forget that it is always possible to change a previous arrangement, and say yes to the person making the request; the key question is whether you say yes from choice or from a sense of duty or obligation. If the latter, once again you will tend to feel resentful and, perhaps, blaming towards the other person.

### *How to say 'No' assertively*

1. Start your reply with a clear, firm, audible 'No'.
2. Do not justify or make excuses. Giving a reason is different from over-apologizing.
3. Feel that you have a right to say 'No'.
4. Once you have said 'No', do not stay around waiting to be persuaded to change your mind. Make a definite closure by

changing the subject, walking away, continuing with what you were doing – whatever is appropriate.
5. Remember you are saying no to that particular request, not rejecting the person.
6. If the request takes you unawares or you have not sufficient time to think when asked, you can always say, 'I'll let you know' in order to give yourself time to think about what you want to say.
7. Take responsibility for saying no – do not blame the other person for asking you.
8. Ask for more information if you need it in order to decide whether you want to say yes or no.

With this in mind here is an exercise on saying 'No'.

Exercise 6.4 (see Notes, p. 133)

1. Think of a situation in which you found it difficult to say 'No' when you would like to be able to.
2. Identify why it's difficult, e.g. 'I'll be letting them down', 'They'll think I can't cope', etc.
3. Confront this possibility in your mind and ask yourself 'Is this really likely to happen?' and 'If it does, would it really be so awful?'
4. Tell yourself what your needs are in the situation and reaffirm your desire to say no in the situation.

## SAYING 'YES'

Saying yes can also be a problem for some people, but is usually much less of a problem than saying no. Consider Jim for example.

### Jim's promotion

Jim had worked for eight years in residential social work with ex-psychiatric patients on their way back to the 'community'. He had spent the last four years as the deputy to the head of a home, who met him for a drink one evening after work.

'Well, Jim, I'd like you to be the first to know. I'm off. I've got a new post in the Hospital and I've given in my notice here.' 'Well, congratulations! Well done, Lisa,' said Jim.

Lisa basked happily, feeling good being congratulated. She liked it. Then she said, 'Puts you in a good place too, Jim.'

'How's that?' asked Jim.

'Well, look, Jim. You're the natural choice for my job. You've always looked after the place while I've been away and made a good job of it. You've got the qualifications and the experience. You're interested, aren't you?' asked Lisa.

Jim felt confused. He had been very happy working as deputy and running the home. He knew he could do the job and he wanted it. Yes, he wanted it very much. Yet he felt confused and uneasy.

'Well . . . er . . . um . . . I'll have to think about it,' replied Jim.

Jim wants the job, yet he has difficulty in saying 'Yes' when he is asked. If Lisa, the head of the home, thinks that Jim does not want the job or is uncertain as to whether he wants the job or not then she is not going to recommend him for it.

There are quite a few 'Jims' around who are 'Always the bridesmaid, never the bride'. If someone does not want responsibility that is one thing, but if someone like Jim does want responsibility but cannot say yes to the opportunity when it is offered then they will be restless, dissatisfied and unhappy. What do you think?

### How to say 'Yes' assertively

1. Say 'Yes' clearly and definitely.
2. Identify why you would find it difficult, e.g. 'I'd be too forward', ' They should persuade me', 'They don't really want me', etc.
3. Examine these thoughts realistically and ask yourself:
   - Do I want to say 'Yes' to this opportunity?
   - Does it really matter if they think I'm 'forward'?
   - Why should they persuade me?
   - If they don't want me then why are they asking?
4. Having clarified these thoughts for yourself then reaffirm your desire to say 'Yes'.

*Why is it difficult to say 'Yes'?*

**I don't deserve it**

If your self-esteem is very low, and you can't imagine why anyone should ask you, then this is what you may feel.

**They might not really mean it**

This may be an extension of the above. You think they might be asking because they feel sorry for you, or because they are being polite. The best thing is to allow the other person to ask and for you to take responsibility for replying.

**I'm not really sure that is what I want**

You may discover it isn't, and then you may feel afraid and the other party might feel angry and put upon.

**I don't have enough information**

You may not be clear what you are saying yes to. So the thing to do is to ask for more information to enable you to make the decision you want.

*Combining 'Yes' and 'No'*

'Yes' and 'No' may be combined assertively to define what we want or what our limits are in a particular situation.

*Mark and Jill*

Mark and Jill are students at college; they are talking over a cup of coffee in the student bar during the afternoon break.

'Mark, would you like to come down to the pub for the evening?' asked Jill.

Mark would like to spend time with Jill but he also had an essay that was due the next day.

'Yes, thank you, Jill. I'd love to, but I can spend only a couple of hours there. I've got an important piece of work to finish for tomorrow,' Mark replied.

'Oh, can't that wait, Mark? Couldn't you put it off till next week?' asked Jill plaintively.

'No, Jill, I can't. It's important to me that I get that essay done.

71

I would still like to come down for a couple of hours though,' responded Mark.

Jill may now say yes or no to Mark if she is assertive, or may agree, and then, when Mark is at the pub, try to persuade him to stay, perhaps by pleading with him. This will give Mark another chance to be assertive. By using yes and no in the way he has Mark has given himself the best chance of getting what he wants and of being respected by Jill.

### Other things to think about

1. We always have a 'gut' feeling as to whether we want to say 'Yes' or 'No'. Remember to take this into account.
2. Not saying 'No' when we want to means that we are placing more importance on the other person's needs than on our own. We are failing to draw clear boundaries.
3. If you do not say no as often as you would like to, think of it in terms of saying yes to yourself more often.
4. Saying yes when you want to say no actually denies your own importance.

Saying 'No' when that is what we want to say is being positive, not negative. Using 'No' in this way is a fundamental and powerful skill in assertion.

Similarly many of us have difficulty in saying yes, in receiving. Often we feel we have to reciprocate immediately, to 'even things out'. If we have sufficient self-esteem, we will accept compliments and other good things and not feel at a disadvantage because the other person has given us something.

Other cultures accept that givers benefit themselves as well as the relationship. From this perspective it is easy to receive without feeling that you are giving away your power.

# Chapter Seven

# DEALING WITH CRITICISM

Most of us become defensive when criticized. We often have memories of being criticized as children, and of it hurting enormously. So we now tend to view criticism as a 'bad thing'. It does not have to be. But in order to differentiate between criticism which may say more about the other person than you and criticism which may be helpful and much to our advantage, we need to be able to assess ourselves. This means being clear about our own opinions of our thoughts, actions and feelings.

## OUR HISTORY

In order to deal with criticism, it is important to be able to assess ourselves. We are not always taught this as children, when our actions are pronounced right or wrong by adults, without them taking into account why we took a certain action or how we obtained a particular result. Children are often brought up to depend on others for an assessment of their behaviour and actions and are not encouraged to have standards of measurement for themselves.

We need to have our own standards of measurement, otherwise we will very easily accept others' criticism of us. For example if you are told enough times that you are too slow in completing a piece of work, even though you know that this pace suits you, you will begin to believe it, and start apologizing for it if you do not have enough self-esteem to make an accurate self-assessment.

Unfortunately we have all imbibed these messages we were given in the past, perhaps by our parents or teachers. There may be some messages we were given so strongly or were reinforced to such a great extent, that we now really believe them to be true. A first step towards dealing with criticism can be to identify some of these messages.

Examples are: 'You're hopeless', 'You're stupid', 'You're too slow', 'You can't do it'. These messages, if taken in, make us feel powerless. You will then be reluctant to admit to being in the wrong, and immediately tend to become defensive when criticized.

Our own standards of measurement which we apply to ourselves all too often do not support us, because of these messages we have imbibed. Often we tend to feel we are not doing as well as we should. We are only too ready to believe we are bad. This is one of the reasons why people find anger difficult to deal with – if someone is angry with them, they immediately feel wrong and hurt and rejected.

Withdrawal of parental approval can be traumatic for a child. And most people grow up with emotional residues as a result of these experiences in childhood. Build-up of low self-esteem as a child can lead to a feeling of not being OK as an adult.

Let us look further at the messages we have been given, and thereby at the origin of our 'Internal Critic'.

First, all too often, our parents have not made it clear that it is a particular piece of behaviour that they find unacceptable, and not the individual child. Thus children are made to feel they are bad if they do not do their share of household chores, or have a different opinion from their parents. And so the foundation is laid for low self-esteem and negative criticism of the self.

Second, if something is repeated often enough, then you begin to believe it. If you are told once as a child that you are not as good/pretty/intelligent as your brother/sister/little Thomas down the road, you may brush it off. If you are told many times, you tend to think it must be true.

Third, your parents' opinion and assessment of themselves is relevant as to how you see yourself. If your parents assess themselves inaccurately – seem to undervalue their achievements, for example, then you will tend to do the same. If the norm in your household is for each individual to play down their good points, then you will grow up thinking that is how it is meant to be.

When we have become accustomed, sometimes over many years, to labelling ourselves in a certain way, it can become difficult to differentiate between what is a label, and what is true – here is an exercise to help you to do that.

Exercise 7.1  (see Notes, p. 133)

1. Think of a time recently when something went wrong.
2. What did you tell yourself?
3. Focus more clearly on the situation, and check whether
   these statements are accurate, or whether they are 'global
   put-downs' (see McKay and Fanning 1987) i.e. wide-
   reaching generalizations not applicable to this particular
   situation.
4. Tell yourself the truth, i.e. report to yourself what actually
   happened, not your interpretation of what happened.

### Sheila's man

Sheila meets a man at a party. They get on well, and exchange
telephone numbers, agreeing to be in touch. She calls him, and
leaves a message on his telephone answering machine. A week
goes by and she still has not heard from him. She tells herself she
is dull and uninteresting and that she made an inaccurate assessment of this man and how their interaction had been. Noticing
that she was putting herself down in a big way, she then asked
herself whether this was a true assessment of herself and the
situation. On being honest with herself, she discovered that it was
not. They had got on well when they met. He had mentioned that
he travelled as part of his work. Perhaps he was away, had been
very busy, or had simply changed his mind. Whichever was the
case, this does not mean she is dull and uninteresting, nor that she
made an inaccurate assessment of what had gone on between
them. You cannot be responsible for someone else's actions.

So remember, when you are being very critical of yourself or
putting yourself down in a big way, stop and ask yourself, is this
true? Is this what really happened? Are there alternative, plausible
explanations?

## WAYS OF DEALING WITH CRITICISM

In order to combat the mutterings of the Critic inside your head,
it is also a good idea to say some affirmations to yourself. These
affirmations need to be based on who you are, not on your
behaviour. You do not have to be a certain way, in order to be a

worthwhile person; it is enough to be who you are. It is important that your affirmations are based on this premise, in order to combat your Critic successfully. Your Critic is constantly urging you to higher and higher levels of achievement in various areas of your life, implying that you are not OK as you are. Here are some examples of affirmations to use:

- I am fine exactly as I am.
- I do my best. No one can do more.
- I am human. I try my best – sometimes I succeed and sometimes I fail. I'm an OK person.

Exercise 7.2

1. Over a day be aware of the negative messages you are giving yourself. Write them down.
2. Write down a list of the 'shoulds' and 'oughts' you give yourself.
3. If you are feeling depressed or low in self-esteem, ask yourself if your Internal Critic is operating.

Exercise 7.3

1. Take twenty minutes to half-an-hour to make an accurate self-assessment, taking into account the following areas:
   - Physical appearance: list your negative and positive traits and features. Include hair, eyes, dress.
   - How you relate with others: in close intimate relationships, as well as with friends and in public situations.
   - Personality: include your qualities, personal characteristics.
   - How you do your job: achievement of tasks, relationships with co-workers, how you feel about it.
   - Daily tasks: health, diet, caring for your children.
   - Mental functioning.
   - Sexuality.
   - Spirituality.
   - Any other category you want to include.
2. Review this list, and ensure that the negative traits you have listed are not total put-downs.
3. Alter the ones which are, for example, 'I'm hopeless at saying no' becomes 'I find it difficult to say no to people I'm close

to'; 'stringy hair' becomes 'thin, wispy hair'; 'irritable' becomes 'I sometimes snap at the children when I'm very busy'.

### *'People have a right to voice their opinion'*

To what extent is this true? When is someone voicing their opinion an invasion of another's space and privacy and an indirect criticism. Let us consider three categories.

### Intimate relationships

Intimate relationships are between partners, parents and children (young or adult), siblings, or close friends. Very often, within this level of relationship, comments are allowed which would not be tolerated in other relationships. However, it is also within this kind of relationship that subtle put-downs often occur. For example 'You're not having another slice, are you? Do you think you should?' (implying that the person being addressed is too fat).

### Friends and acquaintances

It depends on the level of friendship and what is the norm between these particular friends. Between one set of friends, it may be acceptable to say 'I don't think your outfit suits you'; between others, it may not.

### Strangers

If a complete stranger comments on your appearance, for example, this may be considered to be unacceptable, and an invasion of your privacy.

There are two important points to note in this context. First, people's opinions are their personal affair and may say more about them than about you. It is very useful to learn not to take other people's opinions too personally. Second, when voicing an opinion yourself, check whether it is simply that, or whether it is an implied criticism. If so, is it a good idea to voice it at that particular time – ask yourself what purpose would it serve. Are you being assertive? Are you taking into consideration the other person's feelings at that time?

## *Why criticize?*

Why do people give criticism anyway? It is useful to know why a person is doing or saying something: it can help you deal with the criticism.

1. A person may criticize another for a fault which they themselves have, but to which they are unwilling to admit. Thus, the criticism may have far more to do with their behaviour than yours.

2. Someone may criticize you as a form of constructive feedback – because they care about you, or because they want you to know what they think, or because they want to have a clear, honest relationship with you, or because they have a professional duty to do so. If you have done a job badly, for example, would you prefer that nobody mentioned it, for fear of hurting your feelings, or would you rather you were told, so that you could improve your performance in the future?

3. Sometimes what appears to be criticism is actually supposed to be a joke. Be careful with this, though, because barbed jokes can be a form of disguised criticism or put-down, e.g. 'You don't want any more cake, do you?' could be a teasing remark, in good humour, or it could be a criticism about your weight.

Finally, people may criticize you because they are being vindictive. They may be jealous of you in some way. They may want to 'get their own back' or merely have had an unsatisfactory day.

## DEALING WITH CRITICISM APPROPRIATELY AND EFFECTIVELY

Criticism may be useful or useless, valid or invalid, reasonable or unreasonable. It is up to us how much notice we want to take of a particular piece of criticism. Often we tend to take criticism very personally, and even if we know it has little to do with us, we will accept it, just because someone else says so.

### *Fact or opinion?*

Ask yourself if what the critic is saying is a fact which is true, or is it simply opinion? 'You have made many mistakes in this piece of work' may be a fact; 'I don't think that jumper suits you' is an opinion.

However, we tend to overvalue others' opinions, at the expense of our own, particularly if we feel low in self-esteem at the time. In a sense, other people's opinions are their affair, and we can decide how much we want to take them into account.

### Acknowledge or reject

If you think this criticism is valid, acknowledge that to the person who has criticized you. But don't over-apologize and put yourself down. If someone says to you, 'You made a mess of that', and you feel that you did, say 'Yes, you're right, I didn't do it as well as I could have'. And perhaps add a positive statement for the future, such as 'Next time, I'll make sure I spend enough time on it.'

If you don't think it is valid, reject it in no uncertain terms. Listen to yourself when you get a gut feeling that this criticism does not fit; don't doubt your own knowledge of yourself. You might say something like, 'You're wrong! That's not true. I was not lazy: on the contrary I feel I worked very hard.'

### Dealing with blanket statements

If someone makes a 'blanket' statement that may apply to that particular situation, but not to all similar situations, be sure to reject the bit that does not apply. For example, if someone accuses you of always being insensitive, and you feel you have been on that particular occasion, but that usually you are a very sensitive person, then accept only the part of the criticism which is valid. For example, 'I was rather thoughtless in this instance but I know I'm usually very sensitive.' If you say this, or something similar, you are accepting only the part of the criticism which belongs to you and you are not allowing yourself to be put down.

### Inappropriate criticism

Someone who has just met you may voice a criticism towards you, and you may feel they have no right to make such a personal remark, or that it is none of their business. You can tell them this.

## Building self-esteem

Think well of yourself, rather than badly. Give yourself the benefit of the doubt; allow yourself to make mistakes. Constantly build your self-esteem. Consciously try to quieten the judging voice in your head. Notice whether you are judging yourself in a condemnatory way, whether you are simply making an assessment of where certain steps have taken you, and evaluating your present position. As has been made clear, if you are judging yourself in a negative way, you are all the more susceptible to taking others' criticism more seriously than is appropriate.

## Gaining feedback

In certain circumstances, with certain people, it may be appropriate to ask the person who is criticizing why they are giving you that particular criticism. You may learn something about yourself. We suggest that you do this only if you feel you can trust the person to reply honestly and helpfully. In this way, you can gain valuable feedback about yourself. It is the assertive technique of negative inquiry.

## Avoiding self-deprecation

Remember, when someone criticizes you, not to automatically assume it has anything to do with you; you do not have to take it on board. This is called fogging. Do not invite criticism by making self-deprecating remarks, which invite the other person to agree with you, e.g. 'I don't think this is much good, but have a look at it anyway.'

# DEALING WITH OTHER EMOTIONS

Other emotions may emerge when you feel criticized. This is how to deal with them.

## Feeling hurt

One of the obvious emotions which may come up when you are being criticized is feeling hurt, particularly if the criticism is unexpected or if you felt you were getting on well with the person, or if the criticism happens at a time when you had a lot to deal with anyway. It can also depend on the way the person says it. Remember that a lot of people tune in more readily to the negative than to the positive. So they may voice something negative which they see in you but not voice the positive aspects which they also notice. In this case, you may well feel unfairly treated. To deal with this, it is useful to have some affirmations to hand, so that you can tune in to the positive aspects:

1. Use affirmations which build your self-esteem: use them regularly, not just when you are feeling down or being unfairly criticized.
2. Tell yourself the criticism may well have nothing to do with you.
3. Try not to react immediately – give yourself time to think.

### Feeling disrespected

You may feel disrespected if someone criticizes you about something which you feel is none of their business, or if the critic words the criticism in a way that puts you down as a person rather than referring to the particular piece of criticism, e.g. 'You're really stupid' when you've made a mistake. In this case, you can acknowledge your mistake, and reject the piece of criticism which says you are stupid.

### Feeling overwhelmed

Sometimes, when one person starts to criticize another the person criticizing finds that he or she just can't stop. The critic becomes rather like a dog with a bone, and perhaps brings up past incidents to add fuel to the fire. In the face of this barrage, you may feel overwhelmed and hopeless. In this case, an assertive act may be actually to withdraw from ear-shot of the critic. Or to say something like 'I've understood what you said, please stop now.'

Exercise 7.4 (see Notes, p. 133)

1. Recall a time when someone criticized you invalidly, i.e. what was said was not true.

2. What was your immediate thought?
3. Was the thought or message a supportive one (to yourself)?
4. If not, think of a more supportive message you could have given yourself.

For example if someone criticizes you for something which cannot possibly have foundation, do you automatically assume there must be some truth in it? It would probably be more useful if you paid heed to your own experiences or knowledge of what is true.

Exercise 7.5

1. Do you sometimes criticize others for faults you see in yourself?
2. Think of examples.
3. Think of a particular time you have done this which has meant you were being unfair to someone.

## GIVING CRITICISM

### *Examine your motives*

Ask yourself what your motives are. Do you want to put someone down or do you want to give them straightforward honest feedback which may help them and you?

### *Be impersonal*

Label the behaviour, not the person; for example, 'When you don't do your share of the housework, I feel really angry', rather than 'You're really lazy'. The latter is prescriptive; if criticized in this way, people tend to feel defensive and not open.

### *Be positive*

Balance the criticism with some appreciation, e.g. 'I do appreciate how you always put people first, and always have time to listen; but I would also like you to devote more time to that project – at this rate, it isn't going to be finished on time.' This makes an enormous amount of difference to the way the criticism is perceived and received. Most people are closer to rejecting themselves than appreciating themselves.

### Be constructive

If appropriate, make a constructive suggestion as to how the person could change their behaviour. For example, do not say, 'Be more considerate to me', say instead, 'Please let me know when you are going to be late for dinner.' Do this only if the present behaviour affects you personally, or you have a professional responsibility to do so, otherwise this may sound patronizing or dictatorial. For example, if a colleague's tardiness in completing a project directly affects your workload, you might suggest, 'In future, I'd like each project completed within two days of receiving notification of the project.'

### Be helpful

If criticizing someone's work perhaps in the role of a teacher or supervisor, rather than saying, 'That's wrong', try to find out what they were trying to say and assist them in saying it accurately.

### Examine your values

Remember that if you criticize someone else, this is one step away from criticizing yourself, and being particularly vulnerable to criticism in that area. Try to become aware of what your beliefs are about life, the universe and people in general. We form the fabric of our experience through our values, beliefs and expectations about how things are. We tend to regard our beliefs as universal truths. If others act in such a way that indicates their beliefs are different from ours, we have a tendency to criticize them.

Here is an exercise to look at the reasons behind why you give criticism.

Exercise 7.6

1. Make a list of your beliefs about life. For example
   – People should be neat and tidy.

- Everybody wants to get married.
- Most people over 60 want to lead a quiet life.
- If I don't do everything perfectly, I am a failure.
2. Ask yourself whether having this set of beliefs makes you likely to be critical in a negative way of certain categories of people.
3. Ask yourself if you are happy with this.
4. If not, have another look at your beliefs and notice which ones you tend to regard as universal truths rather than simply your personal beliefs.

### Exercise 7.7

For a day, try holding the belief that everyone – including you – does the best possible in all circumstances; that people are always motivated to take action to support their higher good, given what they know at the time. See if this makes a difference to how your day goes. You may well find that by holding this belief you have less tendency to be negatively critical.

See if you can become aware that the more critical you are of others, the more of a tendency there is to be critical of yourself and vice versa. If your Internal Critic is operating, you stand less chance of being able to assess accurately any negative criticism that comes your way.

It all starts with loving yourself. If you can begin to take even small steps towards this, you can change your life.

# Chapter Eight

# VERBAL COMMUNICATION

'It ain't what you say, it's the way that you say it.'

We do not know what the ancient Greeks sounded like when they talked to each other, yet we have plenty of their writings. In writing about assertive speech we have, as authors, a similar problem. To appreciate what assertive speech sounds like it is important to hear it. Previously in this book we have concentrated upon the words used to speak assertively, though particularly in the examples we have indicated how the words were spoken: 'hesitatingly', 'firmly', 'aggressively', etc.

Exercise 8.1

Consider people you know well who speak in an assertive way and observe them in action. How do they do it? When you have completed your observations compare them with our list below:

1. Beginning – the speaker attracts the listener's attention.
2. The speaker faces and looks at the listener so as to keep his or her attention.
3. The speech volume is adequate so that the listener may clearly hear what is being said.
4. The words are clearly articulated.
5. Intonation and stress are appropriate.
6. Speech rhythms, pauses and silences are used effectively.
7. There is an absence of unnecessary hesitations and of non-words and vocals.

Throughout, the words and the non-verbal communications are congruent. We shall now look at these features in more detail.

1. Attracting the listener's attention. In a group this may be done mechanically by banging a gavel or ringing a bell. In front of a class a teacher may simply say loudly, 'Now, class' – words which are meaningless in themselves but serve to attract attention. With one other person the most effective way of attracting their attention is to say their name; a good reason for the assertive practice of remembering names. Thus an effective teacher will remember the names of students. It is easier to say, 'Stop it, Mary' rather than, 'Stop it you, third row, second desk in.'

The assertive speaker also ensures that the listener's attention is in fact attracted before beginning to speak. Usually the listener will indicate this by facing the speaker and by stopping other activity.

2. The speaker faces and looks at the listener. A demure maiden, or any woman in some cultures, will look downwards to indicate her 'inferior, modest, submissive' position. This is not an assertive way of getting a message across. Similarly shy or self-absorbed speakers may hide behind their notes.

The importance of facing and looking at the listener is that they can hear what you say, they feel that you are addressing them, and finally all of us lip-read to a certain extent and feel less comfortable in the presence of a speaker where we cannot do this. A particularly irritating passive–aggressive (indirectly aggressive) habit is for a speaker to start by looking at someone, and then, while speaking to them, looking away. This gives the listener the experience of being rejected, although the speaker may not have intended this and may have looked away simply out of habit or in order to concentrate better on their thoughts.

3. The volume needs to be at the right level so that the listener can hear the message but not so loud that the listener experiences being shouted at. Looking away from the listener or covering the mouth with the hand, notes, or clothing reduces the volume. If someone does not hear the message, then it may help to repeat the message at a higher volume, but it does not help, and is usually aggressive, to shout.

4. If the words are clearly articulated, this is usually more important in conveying meaning than the volume of the sound. Unfortunately the reaction of most speakers to 'I'm sorry I didn't hear that. Would you repeat it, please?' is simply to repeat their words more loudly or even to shout in irritation rather than to speak their words with greater clarity.

5. The intonation and stress are appropriate, i.e. the modulation of the words to convey the mood of the speaker expresses confidence. The mood of the speaker may be angry, concerned or caring, but in any case expressed clearly and definitely – that is assertively.

Emphasizing particular words can be an assertive way of delivering your message.

'**I** will phone you.' – It will be me, nobody else.
'I **will** phone you.' – I won't forget!
'I will **phone** you.' – I won't write or visit.
'I will phone **you**.' – It will be you, no one else.

Also some sentences may be either statements or questions depending on the intonation.

'You like children.' – statement.
'You like children?' – question.

When speaking assertively it is, as we have seen, best to avoid potential ambiguities of this nature. Thus in English the question above is best asked in the form, 'Do you like children?', which avoids any ambiguity. In some languages, e.g. Greek, this is not possible.

6. Rhythms of speech include variations in loudness, speed, accentuation and pitch. These have the effect of making the speaker easy to listen to. The speech also needs to be punctuated by pauses, i.e. silences which in spoken language are much more subtle than punctuation marks in the written language can indicate.

If a person stops speaking, or rather pauses in speech, it may not be clear to the listener whether the person has stopped speaking or not. This may be used, consciously or otherwise, as a passive-aggressive technique.

Mary is talking to John. She is unhappy and angry with him.

*Mary:* 'I've really got some very strong feelings about that. . . .'

Mary now pauses and John may choose either to reply or to wait. We shall see how neither course of action will work for John if Mary is set to entrap him.

*Mary:* 'I've really got some very strong feelings about that. . . .'
*John:* 'Yes, Mary. Will you tell me about them?'
*Mary:* 'Why don't you ever let me finish what I'm saying! I was just going to tell you.'

*Mary:* 'I've really got some very strong feelings about that. . . .'
John now waits to hear what these feelings are but Mary continues.
*Mary:* 'Why don't you say something? You're just not interested in how I feel!'

So John is in the position that, however he responds, by speaking or by waiting, Mary still reacts with anger. This pattern of entrapment is a fairly common passive-aggressive game. How do you think that John could deal with the situation assertively?

7. Vocals, such as 'um, erh, hum', and non-words such as 'really, actually, well', tend to dilute an assertive message and give an impression of hesitant uncertainty. They may, however, be useful, together with facial gestures, to indicate that you as a listener are paying attention to what the speaker is saying. Professionals, working with people, use these vocals in this way where they are helpful to encourage nervous clients to say what is the matter. They are also useful in telephone conversations, where the usual body-language cues are absent.

Assertive speech also involves particular body language which we deal with in more detail in Chapter 9.

Exercise 8.2

1. Again, observe people speaking.
2. See how their speech corresponds with the features in the list following Exercise 8.1.
3. Is their speech assertive, aggressive or passive?

Before considering the assertive use of your voice further, let us digress to cover the important field of regional accents and dialects.

## DIALECTS AND ACCENTS

Regional accents are different ways of pronouncing words common in different regions and among different ethnic groups. Dialect covers all features of speech, including words and grammar as well as pronunciation. Today Britain still has a greater range of dialects and accents than either the USA or Australia. There tends to be a reduction in the use of regional accents, which seems to be caused by travel, radio and TV, education and prejudice. There is also a tendency to adopt American English with the increased exposure to the culture from that country.

## WHAT IS AN ASSERTIVE ACCENT?

The most assertive accent a person can use is the one which they use naturally and with which they are most familiar. This is subject to two provisos.

1. The listener must be able to understand the accent.
2. The speaker needs to be aware that there are prejudices against certain accents. These prejudices may be positive or negative and in some cases are racially biased.

### *Understanding*

Some strong accents are not generally understood except by those people who speak them naturally. Some dialects of English are so different as to amount almost to a derived language, e.g. Broad Scots and Jamaican patois. We suggest that it is reasonable to learn to speak the language in a way that can be generally understood, because it is assertive to take measures to be understood. To do this does not mean that one's mother accent need be abandoned, nor does it suggest that it is inferior, merely not as widely understood.

### *Prejudice*

There are more or less open class and race prejudices and stereotypes associated with accent, particularly within British society. It is assertive to be aware of this and to appreciate that a message given in a particular accent may be interpreted as a different message by the listener.

Psychological research has shown that information given in some accents is likely to be treated as more authoritative than the same information given in different accents. Thus a standard Southern English accent is generally perceived as more likely to be correct than a Northern English one. This may be the result in part of the BBC choosing since 1922 to use English with this accent. Nowadays the BBC uses speakers with regional accents. When these were introduced a few years ago much negative criticism was directed at the BBC. This was despite the fact that the BBC had taken care to use only those presenters whose accents could be understood.

Exercise 8.3

1. What accent do you use?
2. Do you use different accents in different situations, and if so why?
3. Do people understand what you say?
4. Do you feel comfortable with your accent?
5. How do you respond to the accents of other people?
6. Do you have a preference for certain accents?

### On changing accents

You may be better off keeping your accent rather than affecting a new one.

Rabbie Burns, the Scottish poet who wrote 'My Love is like a Red Red Rose', produced his poetry in his native Scottish dialect. When he became successful and famous he altered his accent and dialect and wrote some of his poetry in English. His early poetry is appreciated all over the world; his later poetry is known only to scholars.

## PRACTISING THE ASSERTIVE USE OF YOUR VOICE

You will not be alone; people have been doing this for quite a while. For example Demosthenes is remembered as a famous Greek orator, statesman and warrior. He is also remembered because when he was young he had a weak voice and a speech defect, but he had a vision of himself as an orator. Demosthenes was true to his vision and practised using his voice. He projected his voice on the seashore until he was powerful enough to be heard over the roar of the surf. Sometimes he put pebbles into his mouth so as to develop his vocal ability; he spoke in front of audiences to overcome his fear and embarrassment. At first he was laughed at, but in the course of time he was listened to and became, as in his vision, a great orator.

Nowadays, learning to speak assertively need not be so dramatic. One may employ experts to demonstrate techniques and to provide feedback on the effects of one's speech. One person who has done this is the former Prime Minister, Margaret Thatcher. She was taught to lower the pitch of her voice, a pitch which was formerly described as 'strident', and to modify her intonation to sound less as though she were delivering instructions.

*Improving use of your voice – methods*

1. Assertion training groups
2. Self-help
3. Elocution lessons
4. Speech therapy
5. Psychotherapy

## 1.  Assertion training groups

Assertion training groups will provide you with plenty of opportunity for learning and practising the effective use of your voice with ample feedback from both your peer group and from professionals.

## 2.  Self-help

This means simply practising and receiving feedback from friends and others. The usual provisos apply in that your friends and work-mates have their own interests at heart as well as yours. They may for instance not feel comfortable with you changing as they may feel that they prefer the familiar you rather than the improved you. A tape recorder can be a very useful instrument in providing feedback. You do not sound the same to others as you sound to yourself. The quality of sound is different as you hear sounds from inside your head as you produce them, and these are not heard by an external observer. Also a speaker will, when pausing, tend not to be aware of the pause as a listener, if the speaker's mind is occupied at that point in considering what to say next. Nevertheless a tape recorder is still a valuable aid. For one thing it provides feedback which is more accurate than any that can be given by others. Finally it is a good idea to practise speaking on one's own, so as to learn to relax while speaking. This may be done in front of a mirror; many famous people practise in this way.

## 3. Elocution lessons

These are lessons, often given by (ex-) actors in speaking well. The focus is often on reading aloud from literature, in order to practise rhythms of speech. An acceptable accent and clarity of pronunciation are encouraged. This may now sound old-fashioned. At one time the upwardly socially mobile had such lessons to ensure that they would pass in polite society. The rich and privileged took similar lessons so that they could be sure of recognizing each other. Such lessons may still be useful today, but it is essential to ensure that the teacher knows what the needs of the student are, i.e. to speak assertively rather than to speak in a way acceptable in refined social circles.

## 4. Speech therapy

Speech therapists are trained to help people to alter specific speech defects such as lisping, stammering and stuttering. If a person has such a problem then it is well worth seeking this form of assistance. Treatment may be through the NHS or private. Speech therapy will help to distinguish a specific speech defect from a general problem of nervousness – the latter being appropriately helped by psychotherapy.

## 5. Psychotherapy

Often problems in speech are associated with emotional difficulties and may be helped by counselling or psychotherapy. This can be either on an individual or on a group basis.

We now turn to two modern instruments which require a little knowledge and practice to use assertively. These are the microphone and the telephone.

## HOW TO USE A MICROPHONE ASSERTIVELY

It is usual for people called to speak before large gatherings to be provided with a microphone. This is easy to use and unfortunately equally easy to misuse. The simplest type is a throat microphone which is worn around the neck; once in position its presence may be ignored. The more usual type is mounted on a stand and is usually detachable as a hand-held microphone. If it is intended to use the microphone on its stand, it is important to adjust the height of the stand before starting to speak. A nervous speaker may not take the time to adjust the height; an assertive one will.

With a normal hand-held microphone, hold it about 30 centimetres from your mouth, relax and speak normally. The electronics will do all the work for you; that is what they were designed to do. But it is hard at first to believe that they will, so there will be a natural tendency to speak more loudly than normal and perhaps to attempt to project the voice. Neither of these help and in fact both hinder. It just takes practice to inhibit these natural reactions. Similarly any tendency to gesture with the hand holding the microphone needs to be inhibited. Otherwise the sound volume will vary from normal to inaudible. People who gesture frequently will find this takes practice. Some speakers learn to gesture with only one arm but others find this very difficult and experience their body as being 'frozen'.

A rarer tendency is the fault of moving the head while speaking. Again this results in variations in the volume of the voice. Assertive speakers will recognize what is going wrong and modify their use accordingly. (Additional microphones are necessary for members of the audience who wish to participate in discussion from the floor.)

## HOW TO USE THE TELEPHONE ASSERTIVELY

Some people are afraid to use the telephone. Most of us feel that a conversation over the telephone is different from one face to face. It is; the reason is obvious. We cannot see the other person and so do not have the usual cues based on body language.

A telephone receiver consists of a microphone and a loudspeaker. It is obvious and easy to place the speaker over an ear but one of the most common faults in using the instrument is not to speak into the microphone. With new telephone receivers this is not as important, as they are designed with more sensitive microphones. This can cause embarrassment as they will pick up more background noise or private remarks (even when a hand is placed over them).

### Telephoning someone

This causes anxiety to a significant minority of people but the situation can be handled assertively. Before you start, ask yourself the question, 'Is the phone the best way to deliver my message?' If yes, proceed thus:

1. Decide on the message you want your contact to receive.
2. Decide how best to give the message – what to say – how to say it.
3. Think of a good time to phone, i.e. not very early or very late (what is early or late does vary between people) and not at meal-times or when you would reasonably expect the person to be busy.
4. Relax – dial – relax – listen for the reply and make sure you are speaking to the right person – relax – and say what you have to say in an assertive way – relax – and listen to the reply.
5. Respond accordingly.

### Receiving a call

You are waiting for a call and you feel nervous. So you say to yourself, 'Yes, I feel nervous and I'm going to deal with this call assertively.' Before the call comes consider how you want to react to it.

1. When the phone rings let it ring four or five times – pick up the receiver calmly.
2. Give your name and number clearly and in a relaxed way.
3. Listen to your caller – respond assertively.

*Responding assertively to nuisance calls*

1. Salespeople telephoning on spec – cold calls.
2. Sex-pestering calls.
3. Friends who want to talk more than you do or at times when you do not want to.

## 1. Salespeople

The call comes in the evening, generally just when you have settled down to dinner. The caller does not make the purpose of the call clear and indeed often lies by saying that it is part of a market survey. The products offered are often 'financial services' or the eternal 'double glazing'.

The assertive response is to ask the purpose of the call. Say 'No, thank you' and ring off. Why keep talking if you do not want to? If you do prolong a call when you do not want to, whose responsibility is it to see that your time is not wasted?

## 2. Sex-pestering calls

These are almost always to women. Many are made at random, i.e. the nuisance caller does not know who he is calling. The assertive act is simply to put the phone down; any response simply acts as encouragement. The only reason for listening would be to try to identify the caller if his voice sounds familiar.

## 3. Intrusive friends and acquaintances

These call for the basic skill of saying 'No' and finishing the conversation. You can retain the initiative and call them back later.

*Exercises on using the telephone*

Pairs of people can practise phone techniques while being observed by a third person who can give feedback and advice on improving technique. It is desirable that the trainees are completely out of sight of each other. A screen is most effective: this is the arrangement used by the Samaritans to train their workers. Reasonable results may be obtained by asking the participant pairs to sit back to back.

## *Telephone answering machines*

These take some getting used to. It is wonderful to be able to work and not be interrupted by the phone ringing while also having the option of not losing contact with people who call. But it can be very annoying for callers if you let the machine answer all the time. Also, make sure that your recorded message is short, clear and welcoming.

## *Two false messages*

'I'll phone you'
'Give me a ring'

Some people treat these statements as simply a way of saying 'Goodbye' and this will cause annoyance or upset to those who expect to be phoned and are not, or who phone up and find that their call is not expected.

# Chapter Nine

# NON-VERBAL COMMUNICATION

Body language is the way we communicate with others by using our body. We do this assertively by being aware of what we say with our body, as well as being aware of the messages others are giving us. From this basic knowledge we can choose to communicate clearly, honestly and directly what we want, and what we feel, to others. Let us start by considering our bodies. We can alter some of the features of our bodies while some we cannot even if we want to.

### Height

For men in general height is regarded as a positive attribute and taller men tend to be more successful in terms of position and power. This tendency goes to an optimum height above which the person is regarded as unusual. The belief that, for women, height above average is not a positive feature is a common prejudice. For women, too, height can be an asset.

### Weight

In white British and North American cultures being overweight is regarded negatively. As usual, in matters of body size and shape, men are generally considered to have more latitude than women. Fat people attract negative stereotypes. This prejudice includes being regarded as lazy, unfit and as not looking after themselves. In other cultures (and a few decades ago in Britain) obesity is (and was) regarded as beautiful in women, healthy in children, and as evidence of success in men.

## *Muscle bulk and tone*

Tone is associated with 'good' posture; thus a firm belly is regarded more positively than a pot belly. In men a reasonable degree of muscle development as in an athlete is regarded positively. The development shown by a body-builder may be regarded either positively or negatively but is seldom ignored. In women, any obvious development of the muscles tends to be regarded as unfeminine, although now there is some admiration for female body-builders.

## *Making an assertive choice*

Most of us have a very considerable choice over our weight, posture and muscle bulk and tone. If we wish to appear positively in and to the world and other people, we can make an assertive choice to do so. Likewise we have choice in our hair length and style, including (for men) beards, as well as in the length of nails and the degree of suntan (if ethnically white) and the type and amount of make-up worn.

## BODY IMAGE

Body image is the perception we have of our body. There are two aspects of this: the cognitive, i.e. our perceptions of our size and shape, and the affective, i.e. our emotional feelings about our body. We may feel our body is beautiful or ugly, strong or weak, sexy or non-sexy. Our body image is a very important aspect of our self-image and hence of our self-esteem. Are you comfortable with your body? Are you happy with the way it is, or do you want to change some aspect of it?

There is a lot of pressure to conform to a particular image in terms of the size and shape of our body. Women in particular tend to take on board this social conditioning, and often lose sight of what they themselves think about their body. This becomes lost in the struggle to conform to the accepted norm. Our body is then viewed as an enemy rather than a friend.

It is important to learn to love your body, as part of loving yourself. It is also important to take responsibility for knowing something about how your body works, so that you can know what to do in the event of minor illnesses, and also how to look after it. Sometimes a good substitute for going to see a doctor about a minor ailment would be to do something physically pleasurable such as have a warm bath or walk in the park.

Exercise 9.1

1. Identify three features of your body which you like (for example your nose, hair, legs, smile).
2. Identify three features of your body which you do not like or you feel unhappy about.
3. Say to yourself about these 'I accept my . . . exactly as it is.'

If the things you do not like are connected with being overweight (if you really are), this does not preclude working towards changing this. But first you need to accept how you are now.

## PERSONAL SPACE

Humans, like other animals, require a certain amount of space around their bodies in order to feel comfortable and not threatened. These distances vary with individuals, cultures and the population densities in which they were brought up. For white middle-class suburban British and North American cultures these space zones are:

1. Close intimate – less than 15 cm.
2. Intimate – 15–45 cm.
3. Personal – 46 cm–1.22 m.
4. Social – 1.22–3.66 m.
5. Public – greater than 3.6 m.

Close intimate zone
This zone is usually entered only when a person is also physically contacted.

Intimate zone
This zone is usually entered only by people with whom the person is close to on an emotional level such as relatives, lovers and close friends.

99

## Personal zone

This is the distance we stand from people in friendly situations such as at parties or in having a drink with business colleagues.

## Social zone

The distance for doing business with strangers or acquaintances whom we do not know well, e.g. tradespeople.

## Public zone

Used when speaking to a group of people, e.g. a teacher addressing a class.

Part of assertive behaviour is to respect the other person. This means that it is important to recognize the personal space of other people and not to invade it unnecessarily or aggressively. Personal space may be invaded aggressively in a variety of ways. A visiting relative forcibly embracing and kissing a child does not respect the child's space and is treating the child like an object. Similarly, an aggressive teacher or police interrogator may intimidate a pupil or a suspect by moving into their intimate zone while asking questions.

The intimate zone may be invaded without any aggressive intent, but the message we send may not be the message which is received. Thus a comforting arm around the shoulders of a distressed person may be experienced as a threatening or patronizing attitude and the person may flinch. This is particularly important to people in the caring professions. Usually close physical proximity and touch are experienced as less threatening to both men and women when the person doing the touching is a woman. This is presumably because most of us have experienced more intimate touch from our mothers in childhood than from our fathers. Touch from women is also less likely to be experienced as sexually threatening, as it is usually men who initiate sexual contact, whether welcome or not.

Men also have a tendency to use their bodies in ways that occupy more public space, as for example in public transport. People tend to use shopping bags, coats, briefcases or other property to claim larger areas of space. A woman may use her bag or coat to distance herself from a man who is moving uncomfortably close. When a man and a woman pass each other in a confined place the man will usually pass with the front of his body towards the woman, while the woman turns her back towards him. Generally in public places both men and women will move to make space if they are asked to do so in a sufficiently assertive way.

## INTIMATE CONTACT BY HEALTH PROFESSIONALS

### *Intimate physical contact*

Various health professionals, who may be a nurse, osteopath, doctor or other healer, will need as part of the treatment to make contact with the client or patient in a physically intimate way. How may this be done so that the client or patient experiences the contact as professional and not as sexual? We suggest the following assertive guidelines, using an osteopath as an example.

1. The osteopath explains the purpose of the examination or procedure to the client – what the osteopath intends to do and what sensations the client may experience, and then invites questions.
2. The osteopath ensures that the client understands and has given consent.
3. The osteopath asks the client to prepare and says what is needed. It may be obvious to the osteopath but it is not necessarily obvious to the client. So 'Would you get ready, please?' or 'Would you get undressed, please?' are inexplicit; 'How?' or 'How much?' may be appropriate responses from the client.
4. The osteopath performs the examination or technique with firm, unhurried and definite movements while explaining along the way what is being done. The osteopath is open to comments and questions from the client during the process and stops should the client request this.
5. The osteopath states that the procedure has finished and ensures that the client is satisfied or otherwise. It may seem obvious to the osteopath as to when it is ended but the client may not necessarily be expected to know that the osteopath has finished.

*Intimate psychological contact*

A psychologist, psychiatrist, social worker or nurse may need to elicit personal information from a client in order to provide advice or treatment. This is best done in an environment where the client feels comfortable and secure. Easy chairs in a light, warm and attractive room, with perhaps a cup of coffee, will help to generate the kind of atmosphere which will lead to a productive meeting. The professional will use open body gestures with a degree of physical contact appropriate to the occasion.

## OPEN AND CLOSED BODY LANGUAGE

These are important, indeed fundamental, groups of gestures and body positions. They indicate our willingness to interact and our attitude towards the people with whom we react in any particular situation.

*Open body language*

We are open to interact with the other person or group and feel positive or warm towards them; open gestures should be used by professionals in greeting clients and in encouraging clients to relax and give information. These gesture clusters are also used by successful salespeople and interviewees.

Open body language consists of having the arms and legs uncrossed, hands open with the palms and the insides of the wrists exposed; the body, feet and face point at the other; the face is exposed and not obstructed by the hands, hair or dark glasses; the body is leaning towards the other slightly, but is erect rather than slouched.

*Closed body language*

This indicates that a person does not wish, or is not open, to interact with another person or group. It may be used assertively in dealing with persistent salespeople, often combined with saying 'No', and while dealing with clients making requests to which a professional is unable or unwilling to comply. Also these gestures are used non-assertively by people in stress situations where it would nevertheless be in their interests to be, and appear to be, open to the other people, for example while being interviewed for a job. This can give the wrong impression; the practice of open gestures not only will make shy interviewees appear more open and confident, but also will enable them to feel that way as well.

Closed body language consists of almost exactly the converse of the open gestures. Arms and legs are crossed to form barriers or objects such as bags or files are held in front of the body, which serve the same purpose. Not facing the person, looking away, avoiding eye contact, pointing the body or feet away, and hiding the face behind dark glasses or long hair are all closed gestures.

### Dominant and submissive gestures

These are used to demonstrate to another where one sees oneself in terms of a power relationship to them. Assertively it is important that you are not giving submissive signals when that is not your intention. If it is your intention then various gestures are available: bowing, which varies from a slight inclination of the head to lying prostrate on the ground; for women, curtseying, and for men, touching or removing hats. All of these gestures have the effect of lowering oneself in the presence of the superior. In this way stature is status. There is another group of gestures to indicate that you are aware of a superior's presence, such as stopping talking, getting on or at least pretending to get on with work, standing up or to attention, or simply not 'loafing'. These gestures are particularly associated with school and the work-place.

### Insulting gestures

An assertive person will take care not to give apparently insulting gestures by accident, through not appreciating that gestures have different meanings in different cultures. Similarly it is important to be aware of the gestures made and their meaning by people of a different culture from one's own. Thus the 'thumbs up signal' to indicate that all is well in the British culture is an insulting gesture in other cultures.

## EYE SIGNALS

The eyes have been called the windows of the soul, and it is from the eyes that we receive much information, perhaps more than from any other single feature.

Pupil size is an important feature and is something to which people respond, whether they are aware or not. This size varies with the amount of light to which the eye is exposed. Many of us may remember when, as children, we shone a torch into other children's eyes and watched their pupils contract. In some animals, for example the cat, this contraction is even more pronounced. But pupil size is also under the control of the autonomic or unconscious nervous system. When a person is sexually aroused their pupils dilate and they are likely to be perceived as more attractive. They have 'bedroom eyes'. A person who is alert and/or angry will have small contracted pupils.

Drugs also affect pupil size. Women in many cultures have put drops of nightshade into their eyes so that they look attractive, hence the other name for the plant – 'belladonna'. The atropine in the plant causes the pupils to dilate. The same drug is used today by eye surgeons to dilate the pupil prior to eye surgery. The effect of the opiates, heroin and morphine, is to produce a sharply contracted pupil, the 'pin-eye' of the addict.

Next we turn to gaze, i.e. where we look. Obviously we tend to look at what or who attracts or interests us. However, if we feel that perhaps we should not be looking, we avert our eyes. When we look at people, there are three areas of the body which may be covered by our gaze.

The business gaze covers the area of the person's eyes and extends upward to include the forehead.

The social gaze covers the eyes and extends downward to the mouth and chin.

The intimate gaze starts at the eyes and extends all the way down to the legs.

If a person in a business encounter uses an intimate gaze, the effect will be that the receiver will feel uncomfortable and invaded, generally without knowing why. It is assertive to be aware of, and to use, the appropriate gaze when in different interpersonal situations, as well as being aware of the gaze which one is receiving.

The extent to which people look at each other during an encounter depends on the nature and intensity of the inter-personal processes which are occurring. If the process is intense then the eye contact will be prolonged, and this is independent of the nature of the encounter. Thus two boxers will try to out-stare each other at the weigh-in, while two lovers may be lost in each other's eyes. During conversation it is usual to catch the other's eye before starting to speak and to look at the person while speaking. There is a natural rhythm to this process. It is assertive to be aware of and competent in using this rhythm, passive to look away, and aggressive to stare.

### Directing gaze

It can be an assertive act to direct a person's gaze. This is what instructors do when they point to a particular area or feature of a machine or painting. Similarly if a salesperson is completing a document with the 'prospect' watching the act of writing, then, by removing the pen to eye level, the salesperson can regain eye contact and move to close the sale.

People do not like, or find it hard to interact with, a person who is wearing dark or (worse still) mirror glasses. It is not possible to make eye contact or to know whether one is being observed or not, and this feels uncomfortable. So if you need to wear dark glasses in the sunshine, take them off before you negotiate.

Exercise 9.2

1. Be aware in your day-to-day encounters when and how you look at people.
2. Be aware as to how you are looked at.
3. Vary your gaze area, length, rhythm and intensity of eye contact and be aware of and sensitive to the responses you evoke.
4. Select the assertive behaviours, the ways of using your eyes which suit you and continue to practise them.

## THE SMILE

Most of us like to be greeted with a smile, which we interpret as a non-verbal signal of welcome and acceptance. Knowing this, some people learn to smile in order to greet people whether or not the people are in fact welcome. This 'professional smile' soon fades, and indeed some people can switch on and off their smile with the same facility as an electric light. This smile is accurately interpreted as put on, forced and insincere by most people. Our advice is to be assertive by not smiling at people to whom you do not wish to smile.

A smile may also be used as an appeasement gesture. A passive person who is angry may tell someone, 'I'm angry. I don't like what you said!' but at the same time smile and thus give a mixed message. It is usually the non-verbal message which is given the most weight. A smile may also be required, or expected, of a subordinate when a superior says something that the superior considers to be funny, or when someone in a group makes a joke and the members of the group smile and perhaps laugh. Not to smile in the first instance is not to appease the superior, who may feel disrespected, while in the second case the individual would become at variance with or excluded from the group.

Suppose you do not like racist or sexist jokes and someone makes such a joke. Do you respond by smiling and thereby not telling the truth, or by not smiling and risking your superior's or the group's displeasure? Not smiling may be a very effective and thus assertive way of dealing with the situation. This is again because non-verbal communication is often more powerful than verbal. A verbal protest may lead to an argument, which may or may not be helpful. Assertive behaviour means dealing with people who make offensive 'jokes' in appropriate ways.

A smile is a very valuable signal of encouragement. A student does a good piece of work and the teacher smiles while giving praise. Wise managers will be assertive by telling their workers when they have done well and smiling while doing so. Sometimes a smile may be negatively interpreted by a client. For example a client may describe a particular piece of irrational behaviour, and the therapist may smile gently at the essential humanness of the situation. The client may interpret this as the therapist finding the client's pain amusing, i.e. being laughed at.

## EXERCISES IN ASSERTIVE BODY LANGUAGE

### Real life

Observe yourself and others in real-life situations. Try out different body language yourself and observe the reactions you evoke from others. Respond with your increased awareness to the signals you receive from others, e.g. if someone is sitting with crossed legs and arms and is looking away and apparently bored and closed to what you are saying, then stop, and ask to establish what the other person is feeling. You may then be able to modify your message.

### Assertion training groups

In these group situations there is ample opportunity to try out various techniques of body language as well as presenting your usual body language. The assertion trainer, as well as other group members, will give feedback and advice.

### Mirrors

Practise by yourself in front of a mirror. If you feel silly it may help to remember that many famous actors and politicians do just this.

### Video

A video recording is better than a mirror for three reasons and is often used in assertion training groups:

1. Information is available from different viewpoints.
2. It is possible to concentrate on what one is doing.
3. The feedback comes afterwards and may be viewed several times.

### Control of nervous habits

When under stress, as for example in a job interview, many people will fiddle with their hands, pull their hair or otherwise show their nervousness. These habits may irritate the interviewers and they may regard you negatively as a consequence. There are a variety of psychological techniques for dealing assertively with these habits.

1. Relaxation techniques, such as yoga or biofeedback, to reduce stress level.
2. Practise the habit so as to bring it under conscious control.
3. Develop a substitute habit which is less obvious and disturbing, e.g. twitching toes instead of twitching fingers.
4. Suppress the habit; this is what children do when they sit on their hands.

## CLOTHING – THE MESSAGES IT GIVES

The clothes we wear, like an animal's fur or a bird's feathers, are an extension of our body. With them, as with our body, we give a message to the world. But is it an assertive statement?

The basic rules for assertive dressing are well-known. It is a question of dressing in an appropriate way for each occasion and wearing clothes that fit, are clean, and are in colours, patterns and fabrics which enhance the wearer. There are now consultants available to advise on colour and style of dress, or you can simply observe and feel what suits you best, with advice from friends if necessary. Dressing to enhance your personality and looks is an important part of self-expression and relating to others. Some authors and painters have dressed up in order to get into the mood for their creative activity. Machiavelli when writing *The Prince* in 1513 dressed in his best clothes and wrote a book which is, even today, read with respect.

In some situations the individual has no choice as to the clothes that may be worn, as for example a police officer or a nurse, who have as a condition of employment to wear the appropriate uniform. People need to know who is an appropriate professional in a given situation and a uniform is a ready means of identification. In a hospital environment the white-coated doctor with a stethoscope is immediately recognizable.

If professionals abandon their uniform for 'plain clothes' they are then giving a definite message to other people. The police officer is saying, 'I'm just an ordinary civilian'. Senior consultants who do not wear a white coat are demonstrating their superiority

over their colleagues, even at the expense of the hygienic requirements of the work. Nurses in psychiatric hospitals do not usually
wear uniforms, thus emphasizing the social nature of their work;
a nurse training psychiatric patients in assertive skills would not
wear her uniform. By wearing ordinary clothes she is stressing her
role as teacher rather than as nurse. In some drug control clinics
the nurses do not wear uniform so that their client group
experience them as less threatening and are given the message
'This is not medical treatment.'

As well as a means of identification a uniform also gives an air
of authority to the wearer. Thus many people feel less comfortable
receiving medical treatment from a nurse who is not in uniform.
They may experience her as not a real nurse, or find the treatment
to be at fault in some way. This has been the experience in some old
people's homes, where the authorities were attempting by the lack of
uniforms to create a more home-like, less institutional, atmosphere.

To dress 'inappropriately' or differently is to make a statement.
This may simply be 'I'm unaware', or 'I don't care.' But if
individuals are aware, then they are making a point. Mahatma
Gandhi wore simple Indian dress as a witness of the state of his
country, while more recently Bob Geldof dressed simply in jeans,
T-shirt and trainers wherever he went promoting Live Aid.
Religious groups often wear distinctive dress to symbolize their
relationship to the rest of the world. By dressing differently they
emphasize their difference.

In many situations there is no formal dress code and here choice
needs to be exercised assertively to give the desired message. In a
College of Further Education lecturers may, and do, dress in a style
ranging from dirty jeans, sandals and sweater to formal business
suits. The freedom to choose is real but so is the consequence of
that choice in the perceptions of the individual lecturers by their
colleagues and students.

There are obvious gender differences in clothing and these may
lead to a degree of discrimination. Some women's clothing, skirts
for example, make certain physical activities difficult, or at least
less dignified: a female police officer is required to wear a skirt, which
makes the physical business of running after a thief much more
difficult.

Often, women are expected to dress to please men. In some
offices women are expected to wear high heels and tight skirts to

look 'feminine'. Here an assertive stance is clearly needed, but it has been held that despite the sexual discrimination legislation a woman may be required to wear a skirt for her work, even when this is somewhat impractical. On the other hand women in some more staid professions find it helpful to dress formally or even dowdily in order to be taken seriously by their male colleagues.

Exercise 9.3

1. Be aware of the clothing you wear and the message it gives to people.
2. Notice if and how you respond to people who are dressed differently.
3. Try dressing differently and notice how people treat you.
4. If you feel brave enough, spend a day as a tramp and a day as a person who has a lot of money and see how you are treated when you make requests for goods and services.

As an experiment, the actress Maureen Lipman spent time as a 'bag lady' in London. She was generally ostracized and was not permitted to buy tickets to her own show.

## OFFICES AND CONSULTING ROOMS

The room and its furnishings in which professional people and their clients meet determines to a significant extent the feeling tone of the encounter. A room used for professional purposes may be designed in various ways to be:

1. Client friendly and comfortable
2. Functional
3. Showing the status of the occupier.

The first two of these will be uppermost in our minds when we, as professionals, design our working environment. As a client we would like to be treated in pleasant, comfortable surroundings, which are appropriate to the function of the meeting.

As an example of furnishings related to the nature of the professional encounter, the psychotherapies of Freud and Adler may be contrasted. In Freudian psychoanalysis the patient lay on the couch (now made famous by many cartoonists), while the psychoanalyst sat at the head of the couch, out of sight of the patient. A client coming to see Adler would find a very different arrangement; two similar chairs set opposite each other at a comfortable distance. These arrangements were not merely functional; they made a definite statement about the relative status of client and professional, as perceived by the professional. The responsibility of the client and the therapist in the healing process was also clearly indicated. Thus the patient in psycho-analysis needs simply to lie back in a relaxed but essentially passive way. The client undergoing Adlerian treatment is expected to play a much more active role in the process.

Clients visiting professionals have expectations and make interpretations of the professional's premises. As clients we like our professionals to have premises which are spacious, well-lit, clean, tidy, well-furnished, and soundproof. Excessive luxury may be resented: 'I'm paying for all this!' Likewise scruffiness: 'So they think this is good enough for us!' or 'If this is how the office is, what's the treatment going to be like?'

In formal situations, as when a pupil visits the head teacher's study or when a private in the army is summoned to the commanding officer's room, there is a formal furniture arrange-ment. The senior person is seated behind a desk with the junior person standing in front. This may be relaxed in slightly less formal situations with the junior person being invited to sit. This used to be the arrangement in most doctors' surgeries. Nowadays many doctors modify this by inviting the patient to be seated on a chair by one side of the desk; the consultation then takes place over the corner of the desk. This position appears to enable the patient, or client, to relax and to disclose more information and thus make the process of consultation more effective.

Doors which are kept locked unnecessarily, and the locking and unlocking of doors in front of clients, gives a very negative impression; a client may voice the opinion, 'It's like being in a prison!' Obvious security of personal files and documents, however, gives a positive feel. We all like to see our personal affairs kept private.

# Chapter Ten

# THE ASSERTION TRAINING GROUP

## REASONS FOR JOINING A GROUP

Why might someone decide to join an assertion training group? Here are some of the reasons that participants in our groups have given.

1. 'I want to be better at negotiating, particularly at work.'
2. 'I want to be able to say no, when I'm asked to do something that I haven't time for, or that I don't want to do, like staying late at work.'
3. 'I want to get in touch with what I want and be able to ask for it.'
4. 'I want to share my experiences and feel less alone.'
5. 'I'd like to have more fun. I feel I deserve it!'
6. 'I'd like to have more respect from other people.'
7. 'I want to be able to tell people what I think about things and to feel I have the right to my opinions and the right to voice them.'
8. 'I would like to feel more equal with other people. At the moment I sometimes don't feel like I'm anybody.'
9. 'I'd like to be clearer about what I believe in.'
10. 'I'd like to be able to make my kids behave themselves.'
11. 'I need to know what is going on with my wife. She just won't talk to me.'
12. 'I'd like to be more positive. When I think about it, I realize that I've got lots of good things in my life but I just don't feel positive about anything.'
13. 'I just feel depressed and miserable and I thought this would help me.'

14. 'My therapist says I need to take responsibility for my life. Can you show me how to do it?'
15. 'My girlfriend said I should come. She said it would be good for me.'
16. 'I want to be able to take things back to shops and to complain about bad service.'
17. 'I know I get aggressive at times. I'd like to be able to say what I mean without going over the top.'
18. 'I want to be more confident.'

These are other people's reasons. Here is an exercise to be aware of your own reasons.

Exercise 10.1

1. Relax and imagine yourself living your life in an assertive way, making your own decisions and creating the life you want.
2. Now think about what actually goes on in your life. How, and when, are you assertive, passive or aggressive?
3. In what areas and situations would you like to be more assertive? Make a list so that you do not forget.
4. Consciously make, and affirm, your decision to be more assertive.
5. How will you implement this? What is your next step?

## WHO ARE GROUPS FOR?

*Who may want to organize an assertion training group?*

As a professional, working in the health field with a particular client group, you may feel that a course of assertion training would benefit the people for whom you are working. Often a good idea is to attend a course yourself first, as this will give you a much better idea of what assertion training involves, as well as being a positive and useful experience for yourself. You may decide to have an assertion training course as one of a variety of courses which your clients may follow. Alternatively assertion techniques may be integrated into a course in social skills, or perhaps your clients may focus on an assertive skill with which they experience particular difficulty.

113

If you are a manager (not necessarily in the health or social service fields) you may feel that assertion training could help your workers to relate more easily and effectively amongst themselves. This will create a happier, more efficient work-force. In addition, your workers will be able to deal better with customers, leading to greater satisfaction and perhaps increased demand for your products. Be aware that if you want to retain a submissive work-force, you may lose it following assertion training. But you will gain workers who express their opinions clearly and who find it easier to work co-operatively.

*Special interest groups*

Groups of people with a special interest in common may ask an assertion trainer to organize and run a training course for them.

People who have a particular illness or disability and who belong to an organization which supplies information and mutual support may wish to learn assertion techniques to enable them to convey information about their condition to others in a clear and incisive way as well as counteracting any prejudice against them. Thus people who need to use a wheelchair for moving around may need to tell people that because they cannot use their legs this does not mean that they cannot use their brain. The title of the BBC radio programme, *Does He Take Sugar?* was introduced as being 'Of special interest to disabled listeners'. The title was proposed as being ironic and as making fun of this prejudice on the part of able-bodied people. However, many disabled people wrote in to the programme to state that they were treated on occasion in precisely this way. Part of the problem seems to be the human tendency to talk down to people, in this case literally as well as metaphorically. It may be overcome on the part of the able-bodied person by the simple act of sitting down to talk with a person in a wheelchair.

Various organizations of consumers may wish to learn assertion techniques as members of a group. These organizations could include shoppers in a local area, the tenants of a block of flats, the shareholders in a firm, or the users of a monopoly supplier, such as gas, water or electricity. Perhaps the participants in such a group would want to combine learning about their legal rights as well as their assertive rights in a jointly led group.

114

Members of a minority racial group subject to discrimination by some members of the native population may wish to learn assertion techniques as one of their ways of protecting their basic human rights.

People belonging to a particular church, union, political party or pressure group may all wish to learn techniques to enable them to demonstrate their views in assertive ways. Members of, say, a peace campaign would be particularly interested in expressing their views in ways which were not only non-violent and non-aggressive but also not simply passive.

As an assertion trainer invited to organize and run a course of training for one of these special interest groups there are several questions that you may wish to ask yourself:

To what extent can I act as a role model for this particular group?

Certainly you can demonstrate assertion techniques and give information on assertiveness, but as what kind of role model will you be perceived by the course participants? Suppose that you were asked to run a course for people who rely on wheelchairs for their mobility, if you are not dependent on a wheelchair yourself can you imagine what such dependency would be like? People in the group will know that for you life is different. Even if you try using a wheelchair for a day yourself, this can give you only a limited insight into the experience of this client group.

Are the concepts of assertion and assertiveness training acceptable to the culture and norms of the group?

In a group which has as a norm manipulative behaviour then assertive behaviour will not necessarily be acceptable. In some charm schools (for women) women are taught behaviour which is passive and manipulative. Under these circumstances, it is not possible to teach assertion training as these ideas are not compatible. If a group of consumers perceive the suppliers of goods as the enemy then they may well be resistant to the concepts of assertiveness.

Am I expected to teach skills other than assertion to the group, or am I expected to have special knowledge?

If you were training a consumers group in assertion techniques, there is no reason why you could, or should, be expected to teach consumer law at the same time. Nor is there any reason why you should spend excessive time learning about a particular disability or illness. You do need basic knowledge but the detail can come from the assertion group members themselves. This sharing can produce a very positive co-operative atmosphere and clarifies the role of the assertion trainer as doing just that and not as being the expert on everything.

What is my knowledge of and attitude towards people in the group which has consulted me?

We all have preconceptions and preferences, however much we like to think otherwise. It is important that in working with a particular group we are aware of our prejudices and act in non- discriminatory ways. Is the group one which is commonly perceived by outsiders as having particular characteristics and if so what are these? How do group members perceive their group and themselves?

### Women's groups and men's groups

If you are a person who does not identify with any special interest or minority group but just wants to attend an assertion training course, one of your first decisions will be whether you want to attend a mixed or a single-sex group. Our opinion is that there are major advantages in attending a single-sex group initially. Women and men have different issues which they want to look at, and it is less threatening and provides more opportunity for openness if group members are of the same sex. You may choose to attend a follow-on mixed group, with both women and men present, all of whom have already attended a basic assertion group.

### Group size and environment

Whatever the origin of the group, the optimum group size is eight to fourteen people, in order to be able to give individual attention. A suitable setting for an assertion training group is comfortable and conducive to concentration and efficient working. This could consist of comfortable high-backed chairs, set in a circle, in a spacious, light and airy room, with tables set aside for writing

116

when necessary. Some combination of a flipchart, blackboard or whiteboard, overhead projector, and video equipment need to be available depending on your specific requirements.

### Time frame of assertion groups

An assertion training group may meet as a one-off introductory day or weekend. This can work well and participants may take steps towards being assertive as a result of these groups. But if you are tutoring a group for a day or weekend it is advisable to provide a follow-up group, or at the very least details of appropriate reading on the subject. More usually, and we think definitely preferable, is an ongoing group meeting each week for two to three hours over a period of eight to twelve weeks or longer. This structure gives participants an opportunity to try the assertion techniques that they have learnt in the group sessions in the periods between group meetings, and then to return to the group for advice, feedback, and ideas.

## RUNNING AN ASSERTION TRAINING GROUP

### The first sessions

## Confidentiality

During the first session, emphasize that the group sessions are confidential. This will help participants to feel that they are in a safe environment.

## Self-awareness

It is wise to set the scene clearly from the outset. It has been found that a group tends to work best if participants know that assertion training is not simply a matter of learning and applying techniques. Generally a prerequisite for successful and lasting learning from attendance at an assertion training group is that the participants are willing to look at themselves and gain a certain degree of self-awareness, particularly of how they behave now.

## Making choices

There is a greater chance of lasting change occurring when the participants make specific choices about changes they want to make, and in which areas of their lives, and that they themselves are willing to take responsibility for changing.

## Learning skills

Point out, if necessary, that assertion training is not a therapy. While it is necessary to take a look at past and present behaviour, the thrust is towards learning skills for more effective behaviour in the future.

## Regular attendance

Give participants an opportunity to commit themselves to regular attendance at the group and to take responsibility for getting what they want out of the course. It is disrupting for other group members if people appear irregularly and it is not conducive to the building up of trust. This is a necessary prerequisite for a successful class.

## Mutual support

Encourage them to be actively supportive of each other – to voice encouragement and congratulations when appropriate; perhaps to share about something similar that happened to them.

## Acknowledging anxiety

Acknowledge people for coming. Attending the first session of an assertion training group is itself an assertive act. Participants will probably be feeling apprehensive, particularly if they do not know the others or the trainer. They certainly will not know exactly what is going to happen, and they may have little idea what to expect. There is a subtle line between acknowledging people's fears and discomfort and buying into it through asking little of them but sitting and listening.

## Self-disclosure

Setting the context for future sessions will involve requiring them to take some risks in the first session. This may take the form of a simple exercise involving a certain level of self-disclosure.

## Inter-group communication

Include some pair or sub-group work in the first session, so that participants begin to get into the habit of sharing with each other, rather than always referring their remarks to you as the trainer.

### Individual inhibitions

In the first session, you may want to go round asking people to identify a particular situation in which they find it difficult to be assertive. If doing this, do point out that people have problems or inhibitions in different areas, and something that one person might find easy may be very difficult for someone else.

### Building self-esteem

Point out that being assertive begins with valuing yourself, liking yourself as a person, and encourage participants to use these techniques for building self-esteem throughout the course and afterwards.

### *The next few sessions*

### Success stories

You may find that during the next sessions, people are coming along to the class reporting a 'success'. It is a good idea to make a definite time for relating 'successes'. Suggest to participants that if there is insufficient class time, they make a point of telling someone in the class, perhaps during the break, about any positive step they have taken during the period between classes.

### Discouraging competitiveness

It can feed into people's low self-esteem if they feel that others are constantly having 'successes' and they are not. Encourage each person to be honest with themselves about what is happening with them and to accept it. Point out that it is only from a point of acceptance of what is going on currently that change can occur.

### Cautious first steps

Try to ensure that people take their first steps towards changing their behaviour in situations which are not emotionally charged – situations which they will stand a chance of being able to handle. This is more likely to lead to success, and success breeds more success.

## Reinforcement

Often when someone changes their behaviour, friends or relatives find it difficult to handle. In order to help course participants to cope with this, it might help to set up some sort of support system, e.g. have people pick a partner from the group with whom they can be in touch if they need reinforcement during the week. Do this after the first two or three weeks, when people have had a chance to get to know one another a little.

## Dropping out

Sometimes people drop out of a course because it is not what they expected, or for other reasons. It can be useful for you, as the course leader, as well as useful to them, if you mention that if people have doubts about continuing that they talk to you, rather than simply leaving.

## Having fun

Encourage participants to have fun! Keep encouraging them to support each other.

### *The final sessions*

## Revision and role-play

Revise techniques in which group members feel they would like more practice. Remind participants that if they would like to role-play a particularly difficult situation, which they have not felt able to do before, then now may be a good time. They have learnt the techniques and can trust the group.

## Share and support

Encourage participants to share what they have gained from being in the group and putting assertive techniques into practice in the outside world. Support them, and encourage group recognition, support and praise for the changes participants have made in their lives.

## Variety of viewpoints

If participants say that they have not made changes then gently challenge this if you feel it is untrue. Often other group members may have noticed significant changes and can give constructive and helpful feedback. Sometimes participants will realize that they have the possibility of interpreting their experiences in a different way.

### Feedback and follow-up

What next? Suggest a follow-up course or courses in areas of particular interest to course members. Give information on these to members and receive feedback from participants on what they want.

## *Possible pitfalls*

These may occur and may prevent participants in an assertion training course from continuing, or getting what they want from the class.

### Negative feedback

Negative feedback from people outside the course group. Often people who are close do not want their friend, relative or partner to change; it may feel threatening. If this is undermining a person's own choice to change in certain areas, stress the fact that everyone has the right to live their life as they want to; do some (more) exercises on building self-esteem. Aim to encourage participants to value their own opinion, rather than someone else's, as to what they want.

### Unrealistic expectations

Participants may expect too much of the course, of the trainer, or of themselves. This is one of the reasons it is important to have a small group so that you can monitor each person's progress. Make sure everyone recognizes something they have achieved, some success they have had.

### Partial success

Participants may have been successfully assertive in a particular area, and yet have not achieved what they wanted. Point out that at one level, even so, they have been successful – they have expressed what they wanted to express; they cannot be responsible for the other person's behaviour.

121

## Dealing with put-downs

People may experience put-downs from people who do not understand what assertiveness is and who imagine, for example, that it is a synonym for aggression. It may be worth dealing with these specifically in the group, through discussion or role-play.

## Slow progess

Participants' old patterns of seeing the negative rather than the positive may (re-)emerge strongly, particularly if they do not progress as rapidly as they would wish. Again, encourage participants to build self-esteem and to focus on what they want.

### *Some success stories*

Here are some comments from people about what they have achieved and ways in which they feel their attitudes and behaviour have changed during the life of an average assertion group.

1. 'I think more about myself. I look after myself more.'
2. 'I have more respect for myself and other people.'
3. 'I now feel more able to take control of situations, to feel that I am in charge.'
4. 'I trust my own judgements and don't feel so much need to ask others for confirmation.'
5. 'I ask questions now if I need more information.'
6. 'If I try something, and fail, I'm more likely to think well of myself for trying, rather than put myself down.'
7. 'I allow myself to make mistakes.'
8. 'I said "no" to my mother.'
9. 'I no longer think that experts in a particular field know best about other areas.'
10. 'I'm more able to control my emotions.'
11. 'I'll say "no" now, rather than be a martyr.'
12. 'I take responsibility for what happens to me, rather than blaming circumstances or other people.'
13. 'I feel a lot more confident.'
14. 'I enjoy life more.'

# Chapter Eleven

# CONCLUSION
## *How to be who you really are*

In this book we have covered what assertion is and how the various techniques involved may be taught, learned and practised. In this chapter we show how an assertive approach may become the basis of your life and may take you towards being who you really are. Let us first revise the main characteristics of assertive behaviour.

## BEING ASSERTIVE

Assertion is about being who you really are. Most of us, most of the time, are a very small percentage of who we could be. Part of being assertive is about shifting our focus from adapting to circumstances to focusing on what we want to create. We then learn which steps it is appropriate to take towards that end result.

### *Being assertive is focusing on your goal*

Focusing on your goal concentrates your energy. It makes a lot more sense to focus on your goal rather than to dwell on obstacles or problems which are getting in the way of your achieving that goal. For example a friend has let you down over a small matter, and you wish to tell them you feel annoyed about it. You also want to maintain a harmonious relationship with this person. Here it would be useful to remember that you have two goals, and not to focus entirely on sorting out the disagreement.

It can be very productive to be aware of your overall goals in life. It is particularly useful to write them down, as this brings them into focus.

You may also want to make a list of the areas in your life into which you would like to put energy, for example work, friends, leisure or an intimate relationship. As you become aware of your goals and what is important to you, it becomes increasingly clear which of, perhaps, a number of actions it is appropriate to take at any particular time – appropriate in the sense that this action serves your wider goals. This awareness also helps you to know the difference between wanting something in the short term and taking steps towards longer-term gains. For example chocolate may gratify you now, but does not support your longer-term goal of being slim.

In addition, if you are aware of and focusing on your goal, you will also know that certain actions, while not particularly enjoyable in themselves, are steps towards your desired result. Having this knowledge, you will be able to make a choice to do these tasks, rather than feeling resentful about doing them. For example you may dislike cleaning, but want to have a house or flat which is clean and tidy. Knowing this, and focusing on your goal, you will be able to choose to do the required cleaning and perhaps even enjoy it as you know it is a necessary step towards what you want.

### Being assertive is being self-aware

Being self-aware means knowing what makes you tick, knowing areas in which you would like to change your behaviour and knowing in which ways you are happy with the way you are. This, as we have seen, involves being honest with yourself about what is happening in your life and about what you want. It is also necessary to know your boundaries, when to say yes, and when to say no. Because someone else can cope with doing six things at once, it does not mean that that is right for you.

### Being assertive is being true to yourself

Being true to yourself means following your own path. If you do not know exactly what that is, making choices will help you to find out.

## *Being assertive is building self-esteem*

Few of us believe in ourselves as much as we could. If we do not believe in ourselves and have faith in our ideas, ideals and aspirations, who will? To build your self-esteem:

- Identify the areas in which you lack self-esteem, and find techniques which suit you which you can use to build yourself up.
- Read books which help you to affirm yourself.
- Be aware of negative messages you give yourself and change them into positive ones.
- Identify what you are good at, what skills you have, what your achievements are, your qualities. Make a list.
- Listen to relaxation and self-affirming tapes.
- Tell yourself you are a unique individual, and that you owe it to yourself to do what is right for you.

## *Being assertive is nurturing yourself*

Nurturing yourself means looking after yourself, not expecting someone else to do it for you. This probably involves making sure you have fulfilling and rewarding work; making sure you have enough leisure time and enough pleasure in your life; making sure you are taking steps towards your long-term goals; congratulating yourself for things you do well.

Exercise 11.1

1. Think of three things which you enjoy, but do not make time to do.
2. Plan a time in the next week or two when you will do at least two of them. Allot a specific time for this activity.
3. Do it.

Loving yourself increases your self-esteem and feeling of self-worth. As you love yourself and honour who you really are, you are more able to make choices which support you in creating the life you want.

## BEING IN THE WORLD

There are various ways that people have of being in their world. Some people experience themselves as being acted upon by the world, others as acting on it, mastering and conquering it. Both these orientations view the world as being immensely powerful and individuals view themselves as being comparatively powerless.

But there is another way of being. This involves intelligent co-operation – knowing about and understanding the world as well as oneself – and acting within this context so that the external and internal powers work in synergy. To do this, the person needs, in addition, to have a clear idea what their goals are. This is essential.

People who experience themselves as being acted upon by the world tend to adopt passive techniques for their survival. They will also become angry, whether or not they acknowledge this, and then adopt passive-aggressive or manipulative techniques for dealing with their situation.

People who feel that they must act upon life in order to survive will tend to externalize their anger and behave aggressively without respecting other people's rights.

People who come into contact with natural forces in their sport or work often develop clear ideas as to how to co-operate with the world. Consider a swimmer caught in a current which is taking them out to sea. The swimmer may adopt an aggressive response by swimming against the current, and if they do so they will quickly become exhausted and in danger. Another swimmer may adopt a passive response by giving up and being carried out to sea. Either swimmer may be rescued but they will need to depend on the actions of others to achieve this. Assertive swimmers would swim at right angles to the current and thereby reach safer waters whereby they could swim back to the shore. In other words, assertive people will take action towards what they want in co-operation with their environment.

The often male-dominated pattern of aggressive conquest of the world may lead to its and humankind's destruction. The Green movement seeks to understand and work with, rather than against, the world. This is an assertive way of being.

## WAYS OF INTERACTING WITH THE WORLD

We shall now consider the ways in which individuals may interact with their world. Some of these are

1. Reactive
2. Responsive
3. Proactive
4. Problem-solving
5. Creative.

### *Reactive*

Reaction occurs against something. It is not using energy to work towards what you want. Reaction is a term which is used in physics. When a force is applied, an equal and opposite force is generated. The initial force is an action: the equal and opposite force is a reaction. In relation to people, the word 'reaction' has some of these mechanical qualities in being immediate and opposing.

A person's reaction may be greater than we might anticipate if the force we apply triggers off energies from within the person. The expression 'triggers' is most apt in this context. The fine finger action of squeezing the trigger of a gun results in the generation of explosive and potentially lethal energy.

Another example of reaction is the knee-jerk reflex; this term is now used outside of biology as a general description of an automatic, immediate, unthinking reaction. An example of this happening in personal relationships is if one person suggests to the other that they go out that evening and the other person exclaims angrily, 'Can't you see I'm tired!'

### *Responsive*

This word is used in at least two ways. It has an exact meaning within physiological psychology as that which follows after a stimulus is applied. More commonly, though, the word 'response' is used to describe what a person does following consideration of what someone else has said or done. In this sense a reaction is immediate while a response is considered. In this case what is said is usually intended to fit in with the first person's way of thinking.

We are taught to behave in this way, to act and speak within certain acceptable parameters. This may feel comfortable and safe but it often means that you do not express what you want to express.

As we have discussed, from childhood we imbibe messages from others, and build up a belief system based on our experiences, so that we are no longer open to each situation as it presents itself. Instead of focusing on what we want in any situation, we tend to adapt our actions to fit in with the circumstances or change our behaviour in order to gain another person's approval or give a certain impression.

We often do this because we have been encouraged in this sort of behaviour as children. We have been told that conforming and if necessary adapting to the norm is the right thing to do. Few of us are encouraged to find the 'right' within ourselves.

### Proactive

This means anticipating a situation and then acting before it happens, either to prevent or ameliorate its effects, or even to avoid the occurrence at all. Only the name is new, the behaviour is not. If the weather forecast is for rain, then I may decide to take a raincoat and umbrella with me. If I'm walking in the hills, I take the appropriate survival equipment with me. Anticipation is a very valuable and uniquely human quality. In fact, it is arguably the reason why humans are at present such successful animals. It is an assertive act.

It can be taken to extremes, however, when people go beyond reasonable anticipation to unreasonable anticipation, resulting in anxiety and fear, which people may deal with passively or aggressively. The passive way is one of denial and abandonment to fate, when the person says, quite rightly, 'I cannot anticipate everything' but then goes on to say, irrationally, 'Therefore I cannot anticipate anything.' The aggressive, controlling way of behaving is to say, 'I can anticipate some things'; so far this is rational and reasonable but then the person goes on to say, 'I can anticipate everything.' This rigid controlling behaviour, often enforced by aggression, does not work in the long run.

Proactive ways of being are now recommended as a powerful management tool. We suggest that they appeal because the concepts feed into the illusion that it is possible to control, or predict precisely, circumstances and people's behaviour. We do not think this is possible.

## *Problem-solving*

This is a way of behaviour and being which is closely related to proactive behaviour and hence is similarly popular in some books on the theory of management. A person sees the world in terms of 'problems' to be solved or overcome. Undoubtedly there are plenty of problems, but the world does not consist entirely of problems, which is why we criticize this way of looking at the world.

Many situations may be part problem and part opportunity or may be either depending on one's point of view. The difficulty with adopting a problem-solving way of behaviour is that one will surely find more and more problems to solve. As we have seen, what we focus on expands. Thus if you focus your energy on solving problems (ironically) what tends to happen is that the problem is more likely to expand than disappear. It is essentially a non-assertive way of being in the world leading to aggression or passivity in the face of a world consisting of 'problems'.

## *Creative*

This life-style consists of envisioning what we want, acknowledging where we are now, recognizing the difference and assertively bridging the gap by appropriate action. In our opinion this is the assertive life-style. It is a way of life which enables you to be who you really are.

# NOTES ON THE EXERCISES

The exercises do not have 'correct' answers and are largely designed to encourage readers to explore their own ideas and experience. We list below typical results for some of the exercises in cases where we feel these may help the reader.

### CHAPTER THREE: ASSERTION AND ALTERNATIVE BEHAVIOURS – MANAGING CHANGE

*Exercise 3.1 (p. 22)*

Example A

1. One situation in which I behave non-assertively is when my parents criticize the way I dress. I often remain silent rather than saying I think I have the right to dress in the way I want.
2. Pay-offs:
   - It is familiar behaviour – that is how I'm used to behaving in this situation.
   - I am validated by them for behaving in this way.
3. Disadvantages:
   - I'm behaving like a child, i.e. I'm not respecting myself as the adult I now am. Nor am I encouraging respect from my parents.
   - I'm not asking (or getting) what I really want.
   - I'm being dishonest with myself.
4. What would I gain by being assertive?
   - A feeling of respect for myself.
   - Perhaps respect from my parents.
   - A better chance of getting what I want.
5. I'm choosing to change!

Example B

1. At work with colleagues who have been there longer than me, and

with my boss, when they give me work to do which is not in my job description.
2. Pay-offs:
   - I won't rock the boat.
   - I won't be labelled 'a troublemaker'.
   - Peace – at any rate outwardly, on the surface
3. Disadvantages:
   - I'm not being true to myself.
   - I'm not really being myself.
   - I'm doing more work than others.
   - I'm getting all the jobs nobody else wants to do.
   - I feel frustrated.
4. What would I gain by being assertive?
   - A fair share of the work both in the amount allocated to me and the particular tasks that I'm given.
   - Respect from myself and others.
   - Honesty in relationships.
   - Inner peace.
   - More chance of getting what I want.
5. I'm going to try it!

### Exercise 3.4 (p. 24)

1. One situation in which I feel powerless is when people barge in front of me in a queue.
2. A step I could take to become more assertive is:
   - To tell myself regularly that I am equal to everyone else.
   - To rehearse an appropriate phrase to say so that it readily springs to mind at the appropriate time, e.g. 'I was in front of you.'

### Exercise 3.7 (p. 27)

2. I see it as a problem that I am not able to find time to do all I would like to do. I could choose to see this as an opportunity to prioritize, to be really clear about my goals; to eliminate tasks or activities that are not really serving my wider goals.

## CHAPTER FIVE: USING ANGER CREATIVELY

### Exercise 5.1 (p. 52)

1. The negative message I am giving myself is 'I'm hopeless.'
2. Is this useful to me? No.
3. An alternative constructive message would be 'I am a very capable person.'

You could simply rehearse this in your mind, or you could write it down.

Remember that saying affirmations is not lying to yourself. In fact you are probably lying to yourself in your original statement. Giving positive messages to yourself is tuning in to the truth, bringing the positive to the foreground.

## Exercise 5.2 (p. 52)

1. Some things I feel or imagine I owe other people are:
   Listening time, support and practical help.
2. Some things I owe myself are:
   Love, nurturing, financial stability and good friends.
3. Some things I imagine or feel other people owe me are:
   Appreciation, support, stimulation, love and understanding.
4. I can now take a look at each of these supposed obligations and tell myself honestly whether it is true that I have this obligation or whether another person owes me this particular thing.
5. Is having these ties of benefit to me in my life? No. If I have these ties, it means I am not functioning from free choice. Or I am putting energy into expecting others to behave in a certain way, rather than having them be free to behave how they choose.
6. I can now make a list of obligations and expectations I feel I can drop. I can make a choice to be free to choose and to allow others the same freedom.
7. This enables me to live more in the present, rather than in accordance with obligations from the past.

## Exercise 5.3 (p. 55)

1. I felt angry because I didn't get exactly what I wanted in the shop.
2. What else did I feel?
   I blamed the shopkeeper for not giving me the correct item.
   I also felt angry with myself and called myself stupid for not noticing before I got home. It would not have been useful to have told the shopkeeper that I blamed him for not having given me the right thing.
3. Would any other action have been useful in the circumstances?

What would have been useful would have been to give myself an alternative message, e.g. 'I did my best.' And I could then have asked myself what my goal was in the situation. My goal was to obtain the correct item, and to spend as little energy as possible thinking about what had happened. Thus, telling off the shopkeeper would not have served my wider goal.

## Exercise 5.5 (p. 56)

1. I was angry with a friend who was late for an appointment. I thought I would not tell her because I wanted a peaceful evening.
2. What happened was that I began to be irritated with her about small

things, and we ended up having an unhappy time anyway.
3. I didn't express it.
4. Next time this happens, I will tell my friend that I'm cross because she is late, and perhaps say that I want to have a good evening and I feel it is best to tell her rather than suppress it. I would also tell her what I would like: that she is on time when we meet, or, if she knows she is going to be late, suggest she lets me know.

## CHAPTER SIX: MAKING REQUESTS – SAYING 'YES' AND SAYING 'NO'

### Exercise 6.4 (p. 69)

1. A friend invited me to a social event which she believed I would enjoy. I would have enjoyed it at another time, but on that particular evening, I was very tired and wanted to say no.
2. I found it difficult to say no in this situation because I was telling myself, 'I'm afraid she will feel I'm letting her down' and 'She may not like me any more.' You might ask yourself what these actually mean.
3. She may feel I'm letting her down, but if we're friends, it's unlikely that she'll let it affect the friendship in the long term. And if we are friends, it is extremely unlikely that she won't like me any more because I refuse one request.
4. My need was to have had a rest that evening. To do this would have been looking after myself.

You might also want to say to your friend, 'Do ask me another time.'

## CHAPTER SEVEN: DEALING WITH CRITICISM

### Exercise 7.1 (p. 75)

1. I had a lot to do that day and at the end of the day a number of tasks were left undone.
2. What did you tell yourself? 'I am disorganized. I can't cope.'
3. Are these statements accurate? No. I am putting myself down.
4. I did my very best. I actually set myself up for failure by allotting myself more tasks than I could possibly do in the time.

### Exercise 7.4 (p. 81)

1. The criticism was that I was untidy.
2. My immediate thought was, 'Well, maybe I am a little' (although I know I'm not).
3. This was not a supportive message to give myself.
4. A more supportive message I could have given myself would have been 'Rubbish! I'm a very tidy person'.

# REFERENCES AND FURTHER READING

CHAPTER ONE: WHAT IS ASSERTION?

Easy-to-read popular books include:

Dickson, A. (1984) *A Woman in Your Own Right*, London: Quartet.
Lindenfield, G. (1987) *Assert Yourself: A Self-Help Assertiveness Programme for Men and Women*, Wellingborough: Thorsons.
Phelps, S. and Austen, N. (1988) *The Assertive Woman: A New Look*, London: Arlington. A new edition of (1975) *The Assertive Woman*, San Luis Obispo, CA: Impact Press.


CHAPTER TWO: THEORETICAL ASPECTS OF ASSERTION TRAINING

The development of the concept of assertion training as outlined in this chapter may be traced through:

Alberti, R. and Emmons, M. (1974) *Your Perfect Right: A Guide to Assertive Behaviour*, San Luis Obispo, CA: Impact Press.
Lazarus, A. (1971) *Behaviour Therapy and Beyond*, New York: McGraw-Hill.
Pavlov, I. (1927) *Conditioned Reflexes*, Oxford: Oxford University Press, reprinted (1960) New York: Dover Publications Inc.
Rogers, C. (1961) *On Becoming a Person*, Boston, MA: Houghton Mifflin.
Salter, A. (1949) *Conditioned Reflex Therapy*, New York: Putman.
Wolpe, J. (1958) *Psychotherapy by Reciprocal Inhibition*, Palo Alto, CA: Stanford University Press.

# CHAPTER THREE: ASSERTION AND ALTERNATIVE BEHAVIOURS – MANAGING CHANGE

Fritz, R. (1989) *The Path of Least Resistance: Learning to be the Creative Force in Your Own Life*, New York: Fawcett Columbine. This is a revised and expanded version of (1984) *The Path of Least Resistance: Principles for Creating What You Want to Create*, Salem: Stillpoint. The newer version is also available in paperback (1989) New York: Ballantine.

Fritz is a challenging and original thinker who comes from a background as a composer rather than a psychologist. Often he describes psychological principles as we would like to see them practised. He consistently adopts liberal humanistic principles. Recommended.

Kelley, C. (1979) 'Assertion Response Discrimination Index: Practice in Recognizing Assertive Responses', in *Assertion Training: A Facilitator's Guide*, San Diego, CA: University Associates.

# CHAPTER FOUR: ASSERTION IN THE WORK-PLACE

Back, Kate and Back, Ken (1982) *Assertiveness at Work: A Practical Guide to Handling Awkward Situations*, London: McGraw-Hill.

The work is addressed to managers and covers assertion as a management skill. It is thorough, detailed and written in a formal analytical style. The authors treat the classification of assertive and other behaviours in a way different from that which is usual in that they classify passive behaviour simply as non-assertive while they do not classify aggressive behaviour as non-assertive. This may be confusing to readers until they become used to their terminology.

Butler, P. (1981) 'The Professional Woman', in *Self-Assertion for Women*, New York: Harper & Row.

Positive, creative and constructive. Passive males would benefit from reading it as well.

Fensterheim, H. and Baer, J. (1976) 'Assertion on the Job', in *Don't Say Yes When You Want to say No*, London: Futura. Reprinted with adaptations in Kelley, C. (1979) *Assertion Training: A Facilitator's Guide*, San Diego, CA: University Associates.

This is a short piece but very helpful as an introduction from the point of view of an employee.

# CHAPTER FIVE: USING ANGER CREATIVELY

Bry, A. (1977) *How to Get Angry Without Feeling Guilty*, New York: Signet.

## CHAPTER SIX: MAKING REQUESTS – SAYING 'YES' AND SAYING 'NO'

This topic, basic to assertiveness, is covered adequately in most assertion training books.

## CHAPTER SEVEN: DEALING WITH CRITICISM

McKay, M. and Fanning, P. (1987) *Self-Esteem – A Proven Program of Cognitive Techniques for Assessing, Improving and Maintaining Self-Esteem*, Oakland, CA: New Harbinger.
Far more readable than, perhaps, the long subtitle suggests. Lots of practical ideas for building self-esteem.

## CHAPTER NINE: NON-VERBAL COMMUNICATION

Argyle, M. (1988) *Bodily Communication*, London: Routledge.
Morris, D. (1977) *Manwatching*, London: Jonathan Cape.
Pease, A. (1985) *Body Language: How to Read Others' Thoughts by Their Gestures*, London: Sheldon Press.

## CHAPTER TEN: THE ASSERTION TRAINING GROUP

Kelley, C. (1979) *Assertion Training: A Facilitator's Guide*, San Diego, CA: University Associates.
A comprehensive and valuable book. It provides much reference material for running groups. Tells you everything you want to know and more.
Townend, A. (1985) *Assertion Training – A Handbook for Those Involved in Training*, London: FPA Education Unit.
Video: *Assert Yourself* (1987) Guild Sound and Vision, 6, Royce Road, Peterborough PE1 5YB.
This video shows scenes from a variety of assertion groups including a work-based group, two teenagers' groups, and a group for pregnant women. It also includes discussion on different topics within assertion between Anne Dickson and Andrew Sachs. Very informative, well-structured, and recommended for using with an assertion group.

## CHAPTER ELEVEN: CONCLUSION – HOW TO BE WHO YOU REALLY ARE

Fritz, R. (1989) *The Path of Least Resistance: Learning to Be the Creative Force in Your Own Life*, New York: Fawcett Columbine. This is a revised and expanded version of (1984) *The Path of Least*

*Resistance: Principles for Creating What You Want to Create*, Salem: Stillpoint. The newer version is also available in paperback (1989) New York: Ballantine.

## BIBLIOGRAPHIES ON ASSERTION TRAINING

There are two major bibliographies on assertion training.

Ruben, D. (1983) *Progress In Assertiveness, 1973–1983: An Analytical Bibliography*, London: Scarecrow.
Stringer-Moore, D. and Jack, G. (eds) (1984) *Assertiveness Training: An Annotated Bibliography*, San Luis Obispo, CA: Impact Publishers.
This work has been published since 1977 in four editions. It appears that no update is planned. The four-edition set contains over a thousand references. Unfortunately the book is difficult to obtain in the UK but may be obtained directly from the US publishers.

There is no up-to-date complete bibliography and readers are advised to refer to the list below and the partial bibliographies contained therein.

## BOOKS ON ASSERTION TRAINING

Here we list the most recent works on assertion training, together with the older works which we have found most useful.

Alberti, R. (ed.) (1977) *Assertiveness: Innovations, Applications, Issues*, San Luis Obispo, CA: Impact Press.
Alberti, R. and Emmons, M. (1989) *Your Perfect Right: Professional Edition*, San Luis Obispo, CA: Impact Press.
Argyle, M. (1978) *The Psychology of Interpersonal Behaviour*, Harmondsworth: Penguin.
Back, Kate and Back, Ken (1982) *Assertiveness at Work: A Practical Guide to Handling Awkward Situations*, London: McGraw-Hill.
Bloom, L., Coburn, K. and Pearliman, J. (1980) *The New Assertive Woman*, New York: Laurel Dell.
Bond, M. (1987) *Being Assertive*, London: Distance Learning Centre, South Bank Polytechnic.
Bry, A. (1977) *How to Get Angry Without Feeling Guilty*, New York: Signet.
Burnard, P. (1989) *Teaching Inter-Personal Skills: Handbook of Experiential Learning for Health Professionals*, London: Chapman and Hall.
Butler, P. (1981) *Self-Assertion for Women*, San Francisco: Harper & Row.
Butler, P. (1983) *Talking to Yourself: Learning the Language of Self-Support*, San Francisco: Harper & Row.

Cheek, D. (1976) *Assertive Black . . . Puzzled White: A Black Perspective on Assertive Behaviour*, San Luis Obispo, CA: Impact.

Dickson, A., illustrated by Charlesworth, K (1982) *A Woman in Your Own Right – Assertiveness and You*, London: Quartet.

Fenesterheim, H. and Baer, J. (1976) *Don't Say Yes When You Want to Say No*, London: Futura.

Fezler, W. and Field, E. (1988) *The Good Girl Syndrome: How Women Are Programmed to Fail in a Man's World and How to Stop It*, Wellingborough: Thorsons. Originally published (1985) New York: Macmillan.

Hare, B. (1988) *Be Assertive*, London: Optima.

Hauck, P. (1988) *How to Be Your Own Best Friend*, London: Sheldon. Series: Overcoming Common Problems.

Hayes, R. and Rosen, C. (1987) *Dealing Effectively with Aggressive and Violent Customers*, Luton: Local Government Training Board.

Herman, S. (1978) *Becoming Assertive: A Guide for Nurses*, New York and London: Van Nostrand.

Kelley, C. (1979) *Assertion Training: A Facilitator's Guide*, San Diego, CA: University Associates.

Lindenfield, G. (1987) *Assert Yourself: A Self-Help Assertiveness Programme for Men and Women*, Wellingborough: Thorsons. Originally published (1985) Ilkley: Self Help.

Linehan, M. and Egan, K., illustrated by Calman, M. (1983) *Asserting Yourself*, London: Century. Series: Pocket Your Problems.

Lloyd, S. (1989) *How to Develop Assertiveness*, London: Kogan Page. Series: Better Management Skills.

Morton, J., Richey, C. and Kellett, M. (1981) *Building Assertive Skills*, St Louis, London: Mosby.

Paul, N. (1985) *The Right to Be You – How to Make Things Happen Your Way*, London: Chartwell-Bratt (Publishing and Training) Ltd.

Phelps, S. and Austen, N. (1988) *The Assertive Woman: A New Look*, London: Arlington. A new edition of (1975) *The Assertive Woman*, San Luis Obispo, CA: Impact Press.

Redfern, D. (1982) *Predictors of Nurses' Compliance with Physicians' Inappropriate Orders*, Epping: Bowker.

Schonveld, J. (1987) *Assertiveness Workshops: A Guide for Group Leaders*, Livingston: Lothian Regional Council Community Education Service.

Shaw, M., Wallace, E. and La Bella, F. (1980) *Making It Assertively*, London: Prentice-Hall.

Stewart, J. (1989) *'Well No-One's Ever Complained Before' – or How to Be More Assertive*, Shaftesbury: Element Books.

Townend, A. (1985) *Assertion Training – A Handbook for Those Involved in Training*, London: FPA Education Unit.

## VIDEO ON ASSERTION

*Assert Yourself* (1987) Guild Sound and Vision, 6 Royce Road,
Peterborough, PE1 5YP.
This video shows scenes from a variety of assertion groups including a
work-based group, two teenagers' groups, and a group for pregnant
women. It also includes discussion on different topics within assertion
between Anne Dickson and Andrew Sachs.

## BOOKS ON RELATED TOPICS

Gawain, S. (1978) *Creative Visualization*, California: Whatever.
How to visualize and use affirmations. Very good.
Gawain, S. (1986) *Living in the Light – A Guide to Personal and Planetary
Transformation*, California: Whatever.
Jeffers, S. (1987) *Feel the Fear and Do It Anyway – Dynamic Techniques for
Turning Fear and Indecision into Confidence and Action*, London:
Century Hutchinson.
Lots of practical exercises. Excellent.
Keys, K. (1974) *Handbook to Higher Consciousness*, Kentucky: Living
Love.
Rodegast, P. and Stanton, J. (compilers) (1985) *'Emmanuel's Book' – A
Manual for Living Comfortably in the Cosmos*, New York: Friends'
Press.
Roman, S. (1986) *Living with Joy – Keys to Personal Power and Spiritual
Transformation*, California: Kramer.
How to love and respect yourself and change the negative into positive.
Excellent.
Ross, R. (1985) *Prospering Women – A Complete Guide to Achieving the
Full, Abundant Life*, New York: Bantam.
Packed with gems, this book explains how to attain prosperity in your life
and how to focus on what you want.

## TRAINING COURSES

These are held in many Adult Education Institutes. Courses are
often run within firms, companies, and public institutions. The
authors run assertion training courses.

## RELATED COURSES

Technologies For Creating courses are run based on the book, *The
Path of Least Resistance*. For further information contact Shân Rees
through the publishers.

# INDEX